Postcards from Planet Eldercare
The Final Frontier

pjoriley

Copyright © 2013, Pjo Riley (Paula Riley)
ISBN: 978-0615839554 / 061583955x
Pjoriley Wordworks – All rights reserved, including the right to reproduce this in whole or in part, in any form, including electronic.

Most of the names used herein have been changed to protect the innocent. Any errors of commission or omission are the author's alone.

Cover and interior sketches by Paula Riley
Cover design by the fabulous Lynne Pierce
Text font: Constantia

Also by Pjo Riley:
Atheist in Church – on Heaven and Other Mysteries,
about which one reviewer wrote: "Ms. Riley is a keen observer of human behavior and she gets to the "what" of an issue like nobody I know. Instead of dwelling on why people believe as they do, in her book ... she is content to explore what God belief looks like to believers. While intellectual giants like atheists Christopher Hitchens, Sam Harris and Richard Dawkins have spent years indulging in written warfare against believers, Ms. Riley has the self-confidence and sense of fairness to observe believers with the respect and dignity she demands from others. I am always relieved to come across open-minded and intelligent people among us who can be themselves and allow others to do the same ... this author could teach us something about respect and tolerance—two things in very short supply these days."

More at: http://www.pjoriley.com

Acknowledgements

I need to learn a thousand expressions of gratitude, the better to shower them upon Kate Larue, whose proofing prowess is matched only by her generous heart and hearth; and Lisa Mortara, whose novels I admire, and whose keen assessments and suggestions helped make this narrative readable.

Then there's Jim Riley's veto rights, still in the wrapper. Thanks, Riles.

A parade wave to High Sierra Writers, especially the group of women writers whose camaraderie and support I cherish on Thursday nights and beyond.

This book is dedicated to all those in danger
through proximity to my writing habits,
in this case: our family (the easiest targets), and Deb Lowrey
and Pam Alvey, who truly excel as listeners and sharers.
As my mother-in-law would say: Until you're better paid, Thanks!

And ... to Tenders and their elders, everywhere.

Postcards from Planet Eldercare

The Final Frontier

Into our pine-paneled kitchen stepped my husband Jim, hands framing his face in a pantomime of an Edvard Munch painting, the one with the man who flees screaming into the swirly blue-black night. Of course, his terror was only figurative. He'd been helping his mother prepare for bed.

I turned from the sink full of dishes, and playing to our routine asked: What?

Jim: I'm being *mothered*.

Me: Oh, well. Join the club.

Jim shook his head as if to clear it. He said: I guess it's not that big a deal, but I'm getting instructed to go to the doctor. From now on, I'm not going to tell her anything.

Being an incorrigible optimist I thought *This too shall pass*. But of course optimism can get you into trouble as easily as any other trait.

As I start this chronicle, my 96-year-old mother-in-law (whom I sometimes call Little Momma) has lived with us in Reno for almost a year, indirectly schooling us about which subjects to mention and which to keep under wraps.

Little Momma

From here on, I'll just call her Momma

Our choices often illustrate our growing expertise as caregivers, assistants, companions, aides, technicians, housekeepers, and kin.

I think of us as Tenders. I like the word's multi-meanings, how it can symbolize an offer of payment or the settlement of a debt; how it can represent a soft or yielding texture or something physically weak. There are tenderfeet, tenderizers, tenderloins, tenderhearted, and literal tenders who stoke steel furnaces and the engines of locomotives, all of which evoke our evolving relations with the elder in our household and the requirements of caregiving. I also imagine that a gentle term might counter my natural tendency to balk at obligations of a certain type.

Momma's advancing age and declining health have long been on our short list of topics. For years she exaggerated her home-management skills while we abstained from pointing out how much direct assistance we were providing. She suffers from osteoporosis, osteoarthritis, and macular degeneration, each in an advanced stage commensurate with nearly a century of life. Oh, and she's hard of hearing too.

Lucky are we that she is untouched by dementia, personality disorders, and other negative psychological conditions. She has only what the experts would label mild cognitive impairment, the sporadic inability to process information. Her short-term memory is failing (what a writer-friend's father described as "... record skipping, only you don't know day-to-day what part of the record is going to skip"). Momma uses a number of vision aids and adaptive medical devices. Add a few prescriptions and as far as she's concerned, all is well.

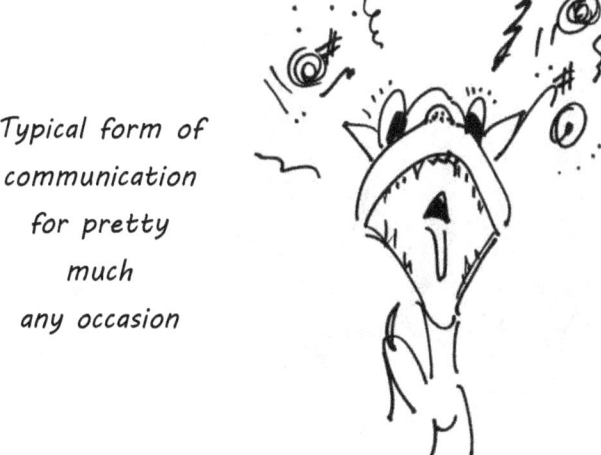

Typical form of communication for pretty much any occasion

Any true misgivings we might have had about bringing her into our household centered on the little dog that has been Momma's constant companion for the last nine years—a ginger-colored female Chihuahua.

This one, who came with the name Gin-Gin, is a yappy sort who has, for as long as I can recall, urinated in a variety of locations within Momma's house. That's the truth, though Momma always protested that her "little darling" couldn't possibly be responsible for those stinky yellow patches on her dining room carpet. "The Rat," as Jim calls her when speaking to me, would face no danger from our big dog, a gentle German shorthair pointer who befriends dogs and people alike.

I've been thinking lately that there ought to be regulations governing the number of yappy dogs allowed to reside within a half-block radius. It doesn't seem remotely conducive to the public's wellbeing to allow a Schnauzer, a Yorkie mix, two escape-artist Chihuahuas, and a mini-mutt to live within shouting distance of The

Rat. There ought to be a law, but there isn't.

Pete— also known as Petie, Peter Pie, and Dogman— with a favorite squeaky toy

We knew that bringing Momma and her hairy friend into our home presented challenges, but we saw ourselves as capable. We had raised a teenager, run a household, and organized sports parties and charity events. I had worked with children and testified in court about the sometimes-grisly details of abuse and neglect cases. My husband had supervised a department staff and wrangled with the Public Services Commission. I had served on boards of directors, and both of us had tutored and mentored young people. We are parents, cousins, aunt and uncle. Retired from our respective careers, we felt we could offer Momma a home with us, should at least try to make it work. Tending an elder couldn't be harder than all those other tasks we had mastered, could it?

Come to realize, eldercare is no job for wusses. For one thing, if you are a woman and the timing is perfectly awful, you might simultaneously experience a liberal allotment of menopause symptoms that dishevel the shape your life assumes. This can lead to strange behavior and curious meltdowns, and I don't mean on your elder's part.

Husbands do wacky things at mid-life too. During what I think of as his early middle years, a man I know bought a Porsche and drove it around for a couple of weeks, parking it at someone else's house between joy rides. Eventually he delivered it to his wife as if it were a gift. She didn't want it.

Jim acquired a red Corvette two decades ago. It was a version of the model he had coveted as a young man and I agreed he should buy it. But that particular car was lousy to ride in and ended up garaged throughout two harsh Nevada winters while his everyday Bronco, which you could use to plow the streets, sat out in the inclement weather. Every winter morning he scraped the Bronco's windows before heading off to work.

Jim said: Is that supposed to be me? (It's true that people look a teensy bit different on paper)

Imagine taking on eldercare while you are menopaustic, which distorts both your waking hours and any potential for quality slumber. Add your spouse's achy back and propensity to talk in his sleep. Is this a good time to assume the care of a person who is falling apart in ways more global than we? Could eldercare possibly be a sane endeavor for medium-oldish people like us? We are used to our autonomy, marital routines, and occasional spontaneity, all of which evaporate on the very first day your mother-in-law moves in.

Still, here we are, and we've done one incredibly smart thing so far—we agreed from the beginning to hire personal aides (also known as home health care aides) to assist Momma for a few hours each day. Having enough help seems the key to making this work.

A few years back we survived remodeling parts of our home, including moving walls and extending sections of the ceiling. Plastic sheeting draped doorways and walls. Workers tramped in and out and we would come home from a long day's work to yet another layer of construction dust coating all the surfaces of our living spaces. There were decisions and details, deposits and timelines. The changes were dramatic but once they were done we liked them.

We survived all the muck and mess, but I have heard stories about couples divorcing during projects that disrupt schedules, highlight money issues, and complicate their inherent differences, inflating minutiae into puffer fish. In that regard, tending is a lot like a remodeling project, only it's not your house you're reshaping, it's your *life*.

For instance, our current bedtime routine includes assisting Momma with tooth brushing, face washing, gargling, donning pajamas, face creaming, Tylenol taking, nose blowing, the application of foot gel, and then the tucking of her into bed alongside a six-pound fury that snaps and snarls at whoever pulls up the bedcovers.

The other night after his turn at bedtime duty, Jim said: I guess I'm just weary of all this.

I looked up from the book of short stories I was reading. He did look exhausted, though not physically spent.

I said: But it's the right thing. That's what we decided.

He nodded: We did. It *is* the right thing.

Me: We'll be fine.

Jim: Yeah.

That's how it works. When he needs to vent, I listen and soothe. When I need to unburden, he makes appropriate noises.

What I didn't remind him was that we are likely to have future duties with my mother. If he thinks what we're doing right now is tough, wait until he helps tend someone who is not his own flesh and blood.

You might be wondering why I would record these details from our shared life with Momma. It must be because writing things down can relieve the "stressors" of life (ask a therapist). Writing down the hard stuff approximates the job of that jiggler thing on top of a pressure cooker. The steam inside escapes as the metal knob does its circular dance, going 'round and 'round, whistling at a pace that prevents an explosion. This chronicle is my jiggler. Also, I hope that through sharing a portion of our story I will better understand the parts my husband and I are getting right, and where we need improvement. Maybe we will both learn a little something.

My husband would tell this story differently. Your chronicles would star other characters and a different plot, but I'm guessing that just a handful of degrees would separate how ours is playing out and how yours will.

↔

Comes December 31. In the last eleven-plus months we have rarely gone anywhere together because doing so requires advance planning to arrange a mom-sitter. This time we agreed to have dinner at one of our favorite local restaurants. For some reason, we hadn't done any deep debriefing thus far. This dinner date would provide the chance to discuss how well we were surviving our extra responsibilities and emergencies. I didn't have a long list of complaints, but there were one or two items that needed the light of a worn-out wife shined on them.

Jim reached past his margarita and my glass of white wine to take my hand. He said: Tell me, how do you think we're doing?

A loaded question. I knew I needed a more equitable splitting of the duties that accumulate during the twenty hours each day that contain no helper-aide. What I needed was my husband to stop scheduling his haircuts or auto servicing or driving range practice at precisely the hour that Momma got up from each day's afternoon nap.

I understood Jim's hesitancy to draw the short straw. He was uncomfortable in proximity to his mother's aged fanny as she rose from the commode to pull up her undies, and he didn't want to help her dress her nakedness.

Embarrassment aside, I needed him to get a grip, to stop leaving most of the hands-on work to me because, well, she's *his* mother, not mine. Hers is the body that bore him into this world. Even if he lacked the recollection, he had once been up close and personal to its most intimate apparatus. Later I would remind him that he was married to someone who would own such a saggy suit someday, and he would need to stand his ground at the sight of it. This night, however, I tried to be fair but direct.

Me: We're doing pretty well, I think. Your mom seems to have settled in. We've got the routine figured out.

Jim: Do we need more help? It's a lot to deal with. You've been an angel. Everyone says that, and I say it too. You're an angel to be doing this.

Let me interject here that I don't know anyone who wants to be an angel when it comes to this stuff. They might want to be a partner or a helpmate, or just good-natured, but an angel? Nooo. The expectations for an angel are excessively grand, and the job description too all-inclusive.

Sitting across from Jim, I took a deep breath and said: Well, here's what it feels like. Things are getting done. I wouldn't say we should have some other arrangement, except … it feels like you're practicing the art of creative avoidance.

Out to dinner, at last, and saying rather un-angelic things

He didn't flinch so I continued: The way you arrange to *miss* the afternoon duties of dressing and hair combing and dumping the commode and snack time.

He nodded, either in benign husband-like agreement or with a dawning realization, and said: I, uh, am I doing that? I don't mean to. At least I don't think I mean to. (He paused.) But I see what you mean. It could look that way.

Me: I'm not saying it's on purpose, that you mean to leave me stuck. But that's what it feels like. Maybe I need to learn to be less nice, less agreeable. Otherwise, I'm the stuck-ee. That's the one part I'm not satisfied with.

Jim: So, I need to get better at checking the schedule, at recognizing what goes on all day.

Me: What I need is to have this be a *shared* arrangement, more shared than it's been so far. I don't want to feel like the Lone Ranger.

He told me that he appreciated all the tending I had done this last year, and that he would get better at coordinating schedules with me and claim his share of the duties. I reiterated that I didn't want to be the schnook, that perhaps I needed to quit being so cooperative, a response he said would not be necessary.

We had dinner then went home and went to bed and got up the next day, which was another day of tending.

I will say that I felt better for speaking my mind, but what really made the difference was my scheduling of time away from the house, what I called "road trips," wherein I would leave for six or eight hours at a stretch.

Let me explain: A little more than a decade ago Jim and I retired from what I refer to as the active duty of careers lived out in corporate offices. Retirement has given me the gift of time to follow my creative impulses. I take freelance writing and photography assignments and in the last few years have begun authoring books. This gives me good reason to spend long periods at home.

In my world, story ideas arrive in the quietude of a sunlit room with a view to sky and a yard of leafy trees. When Jim went out on a typical two-hour hike with his dog, I could sit with my laptop in our family room, where a gentle breeze played through open windows. There I could draft and edit, draft and edit. On a winter's day the view reveals naked trees reaching toward a deep blue heaven.

When my mother-in-law came I fled that space, which being adjacent to the dining room had become the territory of Momma and her aides. That room's soundtrack is now a constant recitation of newspaper headlines and repeated anecdotes about old Reno days and the ancient history of a Texas childhood. As a substitute we rearranged our master bedroom to accommodate an upholstered chair near a south-facing window to which I pull up a tray-table holding my computer. The challenge now is to carve writing time from each day's chores and obligations.

From the outside it may have looked like I was hiding from Momma and her routine of breakfast, newspaper, and the exercises that Jamie, her favorite physical therapist, had prescribed. Well, I *was* hiding, the better to get my own work done. But that wasn't enough; I had lost my happy place. *Ping* went my brain's transceiver, bringing me the answer.

I began to schedule a chunk or two of time away from home each week, otherwise my eldercare duties would continue 24/7. Of course that's what parents of babies and children experience. The parents of disabled children have it tougher yet, Tenders for all their remaining days. And what about the thousands of wounded soldiers returning home from recent wars? Our elder challenges pale by comparison.

Anyway, I don't recall the entrée I ordered during what I later dubbed our *Come to Jesus, Riley* dinner for that New Year's Eve (the best part being that it was cooked by someone else), but that night I practiced admitting that I couldn't do it all. And guess what? My dissatisfaction with our division of duties did not prove our undoing. We are still operating as Tenders, at least for now.

↔

A Late Winter Tuesday ~

Today I ran some errands and when I got home it was almost 2:00 p.m. and the aide was ready to help Momma into bed for her afternoon nap. Their first stop—a health break. The process works like this: Momma parks her wheelchair at the bathroom doorway and switches to a four-footed cane. Whoever is helping supports her hips while she grasps first the doorframe, then the knob on the linen cupboard door, then countertop, then the railings installed on the porcelain throne. From there she can reach the roll of TP and tear off a succession of lengths that are a mere two squares each, none of which would I find large enough for dabbing at makeup, let alone more important business. Such frugality, likely born of childhood years shaped by the Great Depression, dictates that a person might need four sets of two squares, or six sets, or more (I once counted twelve sets in succession).

At Momma's bedside comes the removing of shoes, compression hose, and sweater-jacket or vest. Into bed she climbs, otherwise fully dressed. When she arises later her permanent press clothing will show no wrinkles.

Our aide today was someone I'll call Ellen. We also employ a Pat and a Virgie. I don't know whether we simply got lucky, but we have managed to engage the most patient women you will ever meet. When Momma goes slow (which is always), they go slow. When she repeats and repeats her stories or questions, they join her in the moment. Other than our requirement that she walk a bit and practice some physical therapy, they let her set the schedule. The one thing they can't do is reach for Momma when her dog commands her lap. No reaching for the dog either. Jim and I are willing to take on the beast, which I now call Pickle Dog and sometimes Psycho Dog, but the aides have learned to fear her.

Ellen helped Momma to bed and left the house. I made a list of things I've been reflecting upon lately. During the quiet of naptime I took time to expand my notes:

~*Marrying an older spouse results in older elders.* Any age difference seems a minor issue when you are young, and of course my perspective is not yours. I know a man who didn't start his family until his mid-40s; that's when he found lasting love with a younger wife. When his kids graduate high school, he'll be in his 60s.

~*Southern mannerisms and sayings.* Momma has begun answering "maybe" instead of "yes." If we ask whether she desires a drink, her answer is "Maybe." I had never heard this from her before she came to live with us. At first I would ask for clarification. "Do you mean maybe yes, or maybe no, or you're not sure?" But it turned out she was just speaking the Texican of her youth. "Maybe I'll have a taste of that cake you baked," that sort of thing. An expression of desire through the use of indirection. When she says, "I have an idea about [something or other]" it means she wants to introduce a new topic or offer an unsolicited suggestion.

~*Momma tended her mother for years.* This is not a woman who avoided looking after others. Her own aging mother lived with her for about ten years. Having been widowed fairly young, Momma also handled the financial affairs of her mother-in-law, whose sons were all dead by then. And for years she looked after her own aunt Ennie, traveling once or twice a year to Eugene to assist with projects around the house and yard. This is a woman who has done tending time.

~*Momma once said that people live a long time when someone else is pushing the wheelchair and doing the work.* Her words struck me at the time because I was young and she was referencing the folks in the nursing home into which we had moved her aunt Ennie, a childless widow who had suffered a serious fall while home alone. Before the fall, Ennie had managed fine in the home she had previously made with Uncle Fred. At that point Momma assumed management of Ennie's financial affairs. I'm sure she took that job out of love.

↔

At lunch today I met up with a friend whose mother, 94, lives in Kansas City, her hometown. A year ago DL helped her mother move to an assisted living facility. She validates how hard it can be to live with someone you wouldn't choose as a housemate, how entirely different each family member can be from the others, personality-wise, and preference-wise. She could not bring her mother home to live with her. She could relocate her mother to assisted living or independent living, but not into her own home; they are simply too different. (Her mother is bossy and dissatisfied with much, the exact opposite of DL.)

We talked about whether those traits were evident years ago, or whether her mother had grown grumpy over time. She thought the former. This was probably why years ago she moved a thousand miles away. I admired her candor. She said, "I'm not the right one to do it. I love her because she's my mother, I do love her. But she's not someone I like." She shrugged and let it drop, knowing that I knew what she meant.

I do know. I have long believed that it's possible to love someone and not belong making a life with them. From first-hand experience I can attest that I was not meant to spend my life with every one of the people I have loved, by which I mean friends, lovers and other strangers, and also kin.

↔

Jim's mother was frail when she came to our home just after back surgery for a fractured disk. Talk about medical technology! Her surgeon glued the fracture using arthroscopic tools.

She was also slightly undernourished, a common problem for elders who live alone. After surgery she needed help with dressing and doing simple things. She has experienced other health setbacks since then, but rebounded from them to a remarkable degree. She is one resilient lady. That comes, I suppose, from being widowed young and needing to get tough or get caught in the undertow. She worked until she was eighty, and lived in her own home until it was no longer the best place for her.

People of all ages hunger for self-determination, a powerful elixir. But rare are the oldest elders who can maintain healthy nutrition and hygiene without spouses or relatives to help. We got lucky that Momma needed hospitalization so that we could broach the subject of her declining capabilities (is that actually *luck*?) and that she needed to rehab in a facility or in our home.

By agreement Momma simply didn't go home again. She never said, "I should stay" or "I want to stay." All she said was, "I don't think I'm ready to go home." It was as if she couldn't bear to ask to stay and then not have it work out. She's frail, though, and we felt she should not return to her own home without a live-in aide.

For sixty-two years the house she and Jim's dad bought in 1948 had been her home. It's white with yellow shutters, on a quiet, leafy street in an old neighborhood. Two bedrooms, one bath, and a basement. A one-car garage and along the parkway, gnarled hawthorn trees that bloom a riotous pink in spring. It was enough for the three of them. When Jim's dad died it remained enough for the two of them, and then enough for her.

I imagine that even though she'd spent twenty-five years of holidays and various post-rehab stretches at our house, moving out of her own must have felt like losing a limb. Or a piece of her heart.

With that decision did Momma feel a downward tilt of her life? She rehabbed with us for five or six months, after which we mentioned her unoccupied home and how she might think about staying with us permanently. She agreed, but we could tell she wished things were different.

After filling a massive dumpster with broken bits and useless items she had saved for decades, we held a whale of a yard sale at her house. We collected almost $2,000 before sending 30 cartons of remainders to charity.

The thirty-year-old carpeting had to go. Where it came out of the dining room it was stiff with dog pee. A fresh coat of paint, a new toilet, a good scrubbing, and her house stood ready for renters. Even though it's just down the street and around a corner, Momma refuses to let us drive her past it. I wonder if she imagines that no-one else could love it like she did.

↔

I married an only child. Let this be a lesson. When you marry an Only you become the worst daughter- or son-in-law, also the best.

My first marriage produced no progeny, and once divorced, I had no appetite to produce a child out of wedlock. These days it's not a big deal, the bearing of children outside of marriage, or without a partner or, come to think of it, without an egg of one's own. Had I chosen motherhood, the world would have kept turning through the midnight sky, but I refused to become yet another statistic.

When I married Jim I gained a fourteen-year-old with all the challenges attached to that age group. My saving grace was that I remembered well my own teen years and how it could seem there were too few friends or else not the right kinds, not enough independence, not enough money. Jim's daughter became mine too. I muddled as best I could through my role as step-monster to a teen-in-angst and somehow we all managed.

A future with old people wasn't on my radar back then. Years slid by and then the future showed up and here we are. Fear not, you women who in your early years missed out on handling dirty diapers. There may be opportunities yet.

We began assisting Jim's mother about ten years ago. At eighty years old she had retired from paid employment but still mowed her yard, raked leaves, and kept her own house. Then she fell while mowing and banged her head on the concrete patio. Thereafter, over time, we convinced her to give up her car, then to hire out the lawn care. Eventually she agreed to employ a housekeeper. She needed us, though, for the heavy lifting, like trimming shrubs and weeding the garden. We stripped her bed and carried her laundry home with us, we fetched groceries and drugstore items, we chauffeured her to appointments and ferried her dog to the veterinarian.

She occasionally used her bathtub for bathing, but even with a bench and a sprayer, keeping clean became an onerous task. Pretty soon I was washing her hair at her kitchen sink and setting it in rollers for her. When her toenails grew long I soaked her feet and trimmed her nails.

Because a neighbor had once declared the food "boring," Momma refused to subscribe to the Meals on Wheels program, wherein they deliver a daily hot meal. She still cooked a few items for herself and to give her some variety I packaged single portions from our own meals. Looking back I can see that we were in training, a portion of every week dedicated to tending an elder.

We have another elder waiting in the wings—my mother, who at almost 80 is caught in an inevitable physical decline. She thinks of herself as young-ish, though, at least on the inside.

When she lived only two hours distant I visited many times per year. But since she moved to another state I drive or fly to visit her once or twice a year. I like to think I'm being helpful. There is much to do—hedge trimming, weeding, manure spreading, car servicing, home repair. She resists *needing* help from others, but she says it gets a little harder each year to manage house and yard.

↔

From my notes: The Tolerable Bits
Stacks of printed items on the dining table 24/7
Pickle Dog licking Momma's hands at every chance
Spilled food and drinks
Repeats of repeated questions
Food complaints and preferences; indifference to my cooking efforts

The Cringe-Worthy
Dog who pees on bedroom carpet, thinks she is the boss of me
Dog who acts psycho (all the same dog)
Snotty tissues left on the table
Racist remarks

↔

One day years ago, Momma decided to review her prepaid burial arrangements. She and Jim looked through her records and discussed details. When they were done I asked her if she ever thought about composing messages to leave behind for the people who would survive her someday.

My mental list for her would have included one son, an only grandchild, two nieces, a younger sister, a remaining friend or two. She gave me an unreadable look before shaking her head. Perhaps a shiver of superstition had washed over her, warning that prolonged thoughts of death might beckon it closer.

I am of a different mind. I have long thought about composing letters while sufficiently competent to express a few thoughts. Nothing fancy, maybe something like, You were great. Videos and audio recordings are not my style but something written would do.

In written messages to a few people I could mention just the best parts, and perhaps offer apologies for some of my misbehaviors, the shadows I have cast that admit no light of day.

When I mentioned writing letters, Momma looked at me as if I had two heads. Maybe I do. Maybe one head thinks about stuff like that while the other plans out the household schedule and what we have on hand for dinner.

↔

Now I've got it in my head to write a handful of messages. Somebody once said there's no better time than the present (wise enough words for me). This book can serve as a mailbox.

Dear Daughter,

I'm sorry you had such tough preteen and teen years. No one expects that kind of loss, least of all someone young. It's the children who suffer the most, and the sad thing is that parents know that, even the ones who leave. The leaving is all about the self, not about those left behind.

In your situation I would have felt intruded upon, stunned perhaps, by the arrival of a step-mother of my father's choosing. In your place I might have lobbied to wait a few years longer for the parent who was never coming back, but you loved your father enough to compromise. You accepted the consequences of our love.

Somehow you navigated the years that followed, the high school years, the college years, new friends and new jobs. I suppose your college graduation was a point of pride (you had done all the work, we were simply your boosters), but a later moment moved me more—when your county co-workers said the nicest things about how their team would never be the same after your departure for a change of career. You had been a fair, hardworking supervisor.

You treasured your old friends and stood by them, and became an auntie to their children. You tried marriage, weathered divorce, and discovered that the world still offered love.

I knew from the start you were a good match for law school. It was the right challenge at just the right time for your considerable intellect and skills.

Do you remember that you once surprised me with an offer about my mother? "I can check on her," you said, like it was the most natural thing in the world to look in on someone else's relative, someone you had not seen in a decade or more. Even if it never comes to pass, that was the perfect thing to say. I smile all the way to my toes when I think about it.

I can only imagine your internal life. We are as different as two people can be who through separate acts of love formed a family. I just want to acknowledge how beautifully you blossomed and succeeded and turned out terrific, in spite of the rest of us.

↔

When marketers' thoughts turn to nicer weather ~

An oversized postcard came in today's mail for Momma, one of those direct mail advertisements. This one was from Michael's Reno Power Sports. It reads: SPECIAL OFFER ONLY FOR YOU. Buy a new ... Yamaha or Star Motorcycle and we will send you an additional $300 Factory Direct Cash!

There was more, and I quote: Test Ride a Yamaha or Star Motorcycle and get a FREE pair of Oakleys.

Momma could use new sunglasses. She used to have a pair that transitioned to gray, but those have been replaced by some that please her less. We didn't offer to help her take advantage of this special promotion, though it was kind of fun to imagine the three of us arriving at the dealership with the postcard in hand. You know, just to see how they'd respond to the little old lady in the wheelchair who wanted a test ride.

This reminds me of an article I saved from a *Newsweek* issue, titled "Get the Old off the Road!" It cited a number of dangers associated with older drivers who sometimes head the wrong way onto freeways or mistake the accelerator for the brake pedal.

Motorists have nothing to fear from Momma. Oakleys notwithstanding, she won't ever again get behind the wheel.

↔

Appointment day for the retina specialist ~

Momma asked where her good coat was, the black one she wore last time.

Me: That one of mine that you wear?

Momma: No, mine. The black one with the gray lining.

I got out her black coat with the hood on it.

Momma: Not that one. The *other* one.

I fetched my microfiber car coat with the tan and white lining: This one?

Momma: That's it.

Me: This one's mine, but you're welcome to wear it again. It weighs less than your gray curly lamb you wore for so many years.

Momma: Oh. I thought it was mine.

Off she went in my coat with Jim driving my compact sedan. He drives a 3/4-ton pick-up that even I must use the running board for climbing into, so my car is used for chauffeuring.

Retina specialty care is really something, with high-powered digital cameras for making images of the back of the eye and a variety of treatments for diseases and trauma. To stop the progression of her wet macular degeneration, Momma has been receiving shots of Avastin. The drug, designed to treat cancer, blocks the development of blood vessels, which can end up seeping. The treatment involves numbing the eye, then the patient must hold very still while a long, slender needle delivers the drug to the optical plane. The day after, Momma reports a "gritty" sensation, but that effect diminishes within a couple of days, and then sure enough—the seepage is arrested and her sight improves. Thank the gods of medical research.

↔

My friend KH and I talk sometimes about what happens when childless people get old. There's no telling whether your life partner will still be around so you can dodder together into late old age, helping each other up off the floor and all that. Her blue sky plan is to buy an old motel property and convert it into a senior commune, not as upscale as those places where you get an apartment with a view and gourmet meals, but safe and friendly, and well, *communal*.

If the residents owned the place they could admit only people who seemed sane. Sanity being a relative thing, they might relax the rules about even that, especially if a person under consideration was handy with a screwdriver or a hammer.

If a sufficient number of people bought in, their combined resources might be enough to renovate the grounds and the rooms. There could be a grassy commons and a vegetable garden. Dogs allowed, of course. Perhaps it would be a dog-centric place, dogs so often being the substitute for children.

One problem is that none of us think we are ready to plan such a commune just yet; we all think of ourselves as relatively competent, with many good years left. But most of the local derelict motels are getting snapped up by housing developers. By the time we feel the train of enfeeblement approaching our idyll will probably be relegated to the outskirts of town, far from city services. That means we may have to build a medical clinic into our plans.

KH's mother-in-law lived to a ripe old age. Throughout her nineties the family transported her for lengthy visits to each end of the state where she stayed with her children's families for weeks at a time. KH describes her as tolerant and pragmatic. Never a complaint.

During one of Edith's extended visits, KH rose in the night to get a glass of water and came across her naked mother-in-law trekking to the bathroom. The explanation: sleeping naked precluded any wrestling with a nightgown or pajamas when time was of the essence in executing a health break. Goes to show that in navigating old age, adaptation rules.

Anyway, at about ninety-eight years old, Edith moved into another son's Las Vegas home. While there she discovered penny slots and the music of one casino's Elvis tribute show. She and her son went regularly for those exact entertainments plus the occasional meal. The Elvis band would greet them whenever they sat down front.

At some point she could no longer hoist herself into or out of her wheelchair, even with help. She was just bones by then. The son began carrying her from place to place in the house and sure enough, she made it to 100. For her big birthday shindig, friends and family came from Canada, England, and the U.S. She had made it to a nice round number.

↔

Tools of the Trade:
Pajamas with large buttons
Shoes with Velcro closures
Bath bench or shower chair
Rinse-free body wash
Makeup mirror with magnification
Non-slip bathmat
Physical and occupational therapists
Lightweight facecloths and hand towels
Something to catch the lap crumbs
Gel-filled wheelchair cushion
Old movies and TV shows (think 50s, 60s, 70s)
Clocks and watches with large numerals
Horseradish and other sharp tasting foods
Fruit jelly and cups of applesauce or gelatin
Friends who let you bitch about things
Small utensils, glasses, and cups
Compression stockings
A sense of humor (especially the dark kind)
~ **My detailed product explanations begin on page 120** ~

↔

One March day ~
Today I came across an ex-coworker in Raley's, the supermarket

we frequent. She was buying groceries for her ninety-seven-year-old father. The woman is a social worker whose clients are developmentally delayed and physically handicapped people. Some of them are terminally ill. She shook her head in amazement, saying, "I help all these other people but I'm struggling with my own father."

Isn't that the way? We can support other people, we can empathize and lend a hand, and discuss how to keep elders safe, but in those cases we are dealing with other people's parents. At those moments we feel capable.

This friend's father doesn't want to leave his home, but she's trying to find him a spot in a group home where he'll have companionship and a bit of independence. Someone to cook, help with hygiene, and deliver him to doctor appointments.

He had told her, "Just go get a homeless person who can move in here," or words to that effect. Yeah, right.

The daughter was on grocery duty because she had taken away her father's car keys.

Me: Car keys? He was driving?

KS: Oh yeah! The last time he went to the DMV, back in 2004, they renewed his license so that it was valid until he turns one hundred.

I must have looked astonished.

KS: Crazy, huh? What were they thinking, letting a hundred-year-old drive?

Me: If he's been driving at ninety-seven I'm glad I wasn't on the same street with him.

KS: He likes to go over to Western Village for a meal. He stays off the freeways, but still, that's a long way. He tried to tell me that his cousin drove until he was ninety-seven. I thought, really? That just doesn't sound right, but I suppose it could be. And then I was looking through some stuff and I find the cousin's obituary. He had died at eighty-five. The next time Dad used that line on me I told him I knew better. He just laughed.

She described how her father had gone missing recently and she'd not found him until after 4:00 in the afternoon. He'd been out driving, probably anticipating the loss of his auto privileges.

Me: Does he still have his license?

KS: No. I took that too.

Me: But that might not stop him, if he still has a car.

KS: His car is going to a nephew in Texas. He won't have it.

Our conversation reminded me of a cartoon recently circulating on the internet. It's by someone named Holbert, and it ran in the *Boston Herald* in 2008. It shows an old lady behind the wheel of a car parked at the curb alongside one of those mailboxes on legs. As passersby look on the lady shouts her order toward the slot in the mailbox. "I'll have a cheeseburger, large fries, black coffee..." One of the onlookers remarks, "I'm starting to think re-testing seniors for driving isn't a bad idea."

KS lives on the other side of town but her father lives on this side, so her schedule has been: work all day, drive to this side of town to check on him and see that he has some dinner then drive back to the other side, arriving home at 9:00 p.m. We agreed that hers is a crazy schedule.

She said: It ought to be easier.

She's had a lot of practice with the hard stuff. But enacting changes involving her father hasn't been easy. It's been damn hard.

↔

Lunch with friends ~

An older woman I know is taking care of her partner, a lovely lady afflicted by dementia. When this woman talks about their home life it's with a mixture of irony and dismay. They had long ago promised each other not to let their lives come to this. Should one of them acquire a terminal illness she could simply signal the other that it was time to take her leave. Pills would be assembled by a loving partner for the other's self-directed exit from a painful life.

I suspect they weren't thinking about *this,* the dementia scenario, because who really does? We can all imagine heart attacks and cancer and terrible car wrecks, things that put us on life support, thus our medical directives for Do Not Resuscitate, and No Extraordinary Measures. But what happens when the brain boards a long, slow boat to somewhere far from shore, taking the substance of our loved one with it? That's the emotional pain I detected in her voice, the bad joke that is dementia—Take my wife, please!

My friend's partner would not have wanted a life like the one she has now with its uncertainty about daily tasks and undecipherable cues from people she may or may not recognize. She was someone who had traded on her intellect and been loved for it, which makes me wonder: Is it enough to be loved for one's past more so than for one's present? My friend doesn't ask those questions, but I do, because I could be the next oblivious partner, or the Tender of someone lost at sea.

My husband sometimes says when we talk of such eventualities, "Just shoot me," knowing full well I will not, nor will I hand him a gun. As for me, I have talked of moving to Oregon, not only for its fulsome cliffs above waves churning tank-sized boulders into sand, but for its acceptance of self-determination at life's end. I picture a Land's End as a place that pretty much anyone could recognize while standing there; in contrast, Life's End might be a terminus with no recognizable features, a place that everyone else recognizes except the person standing at the brink.

The woman said, "I've told her she's not to start the dishwasher; we've had problems with the dishwasher. But what happened? The other day I went out of the house and sure enough, while I was out she ran the dishwasher, only what she put in it was Dawn dish soap." She gestured with both hands, shaping the air into loops and undulations. "Oh, the mess. Everywhere."

I Love Lucy popped into my head, with Lucy foiled once again by some quirk of machinery that could not compete with her good intentions—bubbles filling her apartment, her building, the surrounding streets. Bubbles piling up to the moon.

We laughed. "Yes," she said. "First you cry and later you laugh." She has posted a sign on the dishwasher's placid face to warn away her beloved. **Do Not Start This!**

But she's too late. The things she doesn't want started are already gaining steam.

↔

April 1 ~

Here I am, fifty-five, and death is on my mind. Not necessarily my own death, but death in general. Maybe that's because friends and relatives of friends and old workmates keep falling by the wayside. Plus, I'm in proximity to someone approaching death at close range (which might also apply to me).

Momma, though, avoids any talk about death, except for scanning the obituaries every day and mentioning whether she knows someone listed there. No discussion of her own mortality or what she thinks about what might come next.

I don't recall knowing much about death in my youth unless it touched someone in the news, President Kennedy for instance. In second grade, though, a neighbor friend of mine was killed in an auto accident. Karen was her name. I knew her well enough to miss her a little, but not enough to know in what ways my life might be diminished without her.

I don't recall my parents' reaction. My mother delivered the news that I would not be attending the funeral. She had probably judged me too young for such an affair, or maybe it was out of deference to how the presence of an intact, living neighbor child might magnify the sorrow of those grieving parents. All speculation on my part. Some things we never know the *why* of.

↔

There appears to be no greater pleasure for Momma than spending two hours with her magnifier and the morning paper; also mail order catalogues and fashion advertisements. In the evening she might read one of the large print novels we buy for her through bookstores or Friends of the Library, which sells donated books to benefit our county libraries.

A close second is receiving a thorough licking of her knobbly hands by her stinker pie dog. They are both partial to sunbathing, Momma with her back to the slanting sun while holding The Rat in her lap. Whichever aide is on duty sits nearby in the shade, sweating.

Momma is easily entertained, content to watch television, happy with Judge Judy, Storage Wars, Gold Rush, Little House on the Prairie, and American Pickers. No matter that it's the same episode as last night or last week, they're all new to her.

"Zeopardy," as she calls it, that long-running television game show, moves too fast against a complicated stage set. She often cannot tell commercials from shows, but will watch almost anything that's on, even golf. Afterwards, though, she might say how silly a movie was. The way the cable channels work, chances are she'll choose to watch the same silly movies again next month.

↔

Said Ellen, the aide, to Momma: Do you want a snack or anything?

They were sitting at the dining table reading the newspaper, normally a two-hour affair.

From the kitchen I could hear the exchange.

Momma: No. I really don't like to eat between meals.

For an instant I could have channeled my mother and interrupted what I saw as a blatant inaccuracy, but I kept my trap shut.

This is because one time I was in the living room of my grandparent's house talking with Grandma, who was in her 90s. Mother was in the kitchen, just a dozen steps down a hall that acts like a sound tunnel. I knew everyone could hear our conversation but I wanted Grandma to have the chance to converse instead of sitting silent.

Mother had taken to answering for her father, who years before had had a stroke. He couldn't any longer conjure sentences a person could understand, though he could say "Shit" loud and clear. They call that aphasia—not the use of swear words but the ability to understand without being able to speak—so my mother had become quite the answerer. Grandmother, though, was a quiet soul by nature, and an acquiescing type. My mind attributes that to Grandpa commanding most of their conversations throughout their marriage.

Unconcerned with fact-checking, I asked questions and waited for replies, communing across our generation gap. Question after question I asked. To each of Grandma's answers came an amended answer shouted from the kitchen.

I was speaking loudly to accommodate my grandmother's poor hearing. Over and over came the corrections. I maintained eye contact and tried to shut out the interference.

Mother and I came to words after she stomped down the hall to let me know that her mother wasn't answering accurately. I said something like, "It doesn't matter. We're just talking." My mother huffed away and I thought to myself, "You have taken on too large a job here and it has worn you out."

↔

I find it humorous that Jim, a man who weathered the sweat and piss of both Army boot camp and armor training, hates to dump his mother's commode bucket, which contains the same stuff of everyday life, just in a different container. But hate it he does (which does not get him out of the duty).

As long as I am tattling: He has little patience for how long it takes Momma to button her pajamas, which admittedly can feel like watching someone thread a fish through a needle. Even if it takes her twenty seconds per button, she perseveres, and with rarely a swear word.

And then there is her hawking and spitting after a dose of mouthwash. For a woman with minimal lung power she can sound like a dockworker. Jim parodies her to me afterwards; that's how I know it bothers him.

In response I simply roll my eyes and wonder which of my quirks he will mock someday.

↔

May musings ~

I've been thinking about how I may ruin this tending experience through overconfidence. I've always had an *I can do this* attitude, which comes in handy for things like attempting a soufflé or changing out a sink faucet. I admit, though, that it may not be the sanest perspective.

Perhaps I should have been more circumspect about tending Momma. Then again, it's not about liking the occupation of Tender. I don't *like* tending, per se, not the way I like solitude, or chocolate chip cookies made with oatmeal and those little English toffee bits. Tending is about humanely executing necessary tasks.

Even though it's his mom, Jim sometimes has second thoughts. When helping me clean up after a bathroom emergency he might say, "If this becomes a regular problem we might not be able to keep her here," to which I've been known to reply, "Maybe at that point we will just need more help." Have I mentioned that I might not be sane?

↔

June ~

Up at 12:30 a.m. with Pickle Dog, whose coloring has changed over time. At first she developed a pale stripe down her back. Then her entire coat faded to the color of straw.

A warning about Chihuahuas: Never let one into your home, not even if it's your elder's best friend. We've known a number of them and they're all the same—extremely loyal and practically brainless. At least think hard about how they are known to have a bladder the size of a garbanzo bean. They will pee and poop any old place. I'm just saying...

When Momma stayed with us the first January after her back surgery, we tied a bell to her hospital-style bed so that she could summon us for help. We've been hearing it virtually every night since, but on rare occasions is it for Momma herself. Mostly we get rung to let Pickle Dog out. That's because we don't have a doggie door, not that she'd be smart enough to use one.

I never bore babies, never responded to an infant's cry in the night, but from across a hall and through a closed solid-wood door that bell can rouse me from the fog of a deep dream. I even sometimes wake to the jingle of Pickle Dog's collar as she stands on Momma's bed and shakes. Conversely, my husband, who has poor hearing after five-plus decades of hunting with a shotgun, cannot hear that high-toned bell.

Here's an insight derived from empirical evidence: Twelve-year-old Chihuahuas can't digest nuts. Unfortunately, nuts don't kill them or I'd feed her some myself. They mostly come out the other end intact. So each time I see the stinker's poop studded like some alien lawn fudge I suggest to Momma *once again* that maybe nuts aren't such a good snack to share with her aging dog. Momma nods sagely in agreement, but when she gets engrossed in watching Judge Judy rail against the so-called "stupid" plaintiffs and defendants who daily come before her, Momma's little love bug gets to snack on nuts.

↔

August ~

At ninety, a person might feel entitled to have a birthday dinner or a nice cake or something.

Momma always says she never had a birthday when she was young. She means that during her childhood, her family didn't celebrate by throwing parties. I'm sure that's the case but as far as I can tell from her stories, they didn't go hungry; in fact, when "hoboes" came around to the back door, her mother always rustled up a sandwich or other food to give them.

As Momma hit milestone years, and for some of her birthdays in between, we gathered our immediate family and her closest friends for brunch or dinner, because what if it proved to be the last one?

We've arrived at 96 and I'm still thinking, What if it's the last one? This time Momma actually asked for a birthday dinner, so we obliged.

Being concerned about the location of bathrooms in her favorite local restaurant, she opted for a family dinner on the deck at home.

We fetched frog legs from Simon's Restaurant and served them as appetizers. The rest came from our kitchen and grill. The weather was warm and fine. If it proves to be Momma's last celebration, we will have marked the year.

↔

Second week of September ~

We seem to be traveling smooth waters right now so I have been getting a little time away from the house. For people who go to an office, working from home, even if spent at a computer screen or making business calls, might seem like getting away from official duties.

As someone who works from home, any hours I spend at my laptop occur in the same location as the hours spent as Tender. Consequently even errands have taken on an attractive glow of *away-ness* that can provide a break in the day. Said running about needs to be accomplished while one of the aides is in residence (10:00 a.m.–2:00 p.m.) or else when my husband is "on duty," as we call it.

Even so, on a bright day it's good to get out with NPR on the car radio, no distant chime of the washer or dryer, and no duplicate or triplicate questions of "What's on your agenda today?"

I am learning to be gladder than ever for the little things.

↔

Now that we have an elder counting on breakfast, plus a snack, plus dinner, there is no getting out of the occasional meal by refusing to cook, or by skipping out to a restaurant. A couple of truths about me: I contain no genes for the desire to cook, and I don't care all that much about food. Well ... I do like a nice meal of simple food and fresh flavors, but cooking is my least favorite activity. I'd rather sweep the deck. I'd rather wash the car. Hell, I'd rather spend an hour pulling weeds than in the kitchen. Also, I'm not all that excited about dining out, though local food offerings are plentiful and varied. I'm more of a "lunch out" person, and a semi-regular one at that. The bottom line is: Except for very few occasions spread thinly throughout the year, I lack the desire to linger in the kitchen.

Jim is a man of many talents. Cooking is not one of them, though he can grill pretty much anything. He wrenches open a jar of Ragu with the best of them and scrambles a fine egg, but he's like me in that he'd rather not be charged with such mundane affairs. I do know women whose husbands love to cook and I always praise them for choosing well.

My husband, on the other hand, is simply avoiding mutiny when he assumes a share of the cooking duties, per our agreement from years back, which itself arose after I grew weary of my tenure as the default cook.

You may know people who like to wait on others. I'm sure I know a few, the sort of person who feels fulfilled through serving as chef, laundress, social secretary, housekeeper, organizer, shopper, fixer, wrapper, repairman, seamstress, and chronicler of daily life. I grew up in a traditional household where it was a woman's job to execute the majority of those roles while the man brought home the proverbial bacon. Being the only girl among four siblings, I was assigned the scrubbing of toilets plus vacuuming and dusting, which from an early age felt to me like being a maid while the boys got to be the landscaping crew and handlers of hammers and other cool tools.

Though I disliked that lopsided division of duties I operated much along those lines when I first set out in life; it's what I knew. Only later did I recognize how little I enjoy waiting on others who are perfectly capable of performing the same household tasks as I, but don't.

Out of self-preservation I now acquiesce to using more take-out and prepared foods. The rest of the working world has probably always relied on little helpers such as roasted chickens from the deli, or pre-sauced ribs, or ready-to-eat shrimp. I held out until this year.

We have different food preferences than Momma, whose taste buds have gone the way of her high heeled shoes—mere memories now. Still, she likes to eat what she's always eaten, the regulars being beef and potatoes, whereas Jim and I could live long stretches without beef; we like all manner of fish, which she would never choose.

My al dente vegetables elicit complaints, so sometimes I offer her a serving of canned veggies (sure to resemble pulp), but then she claims they're bland, in spite of all the sodium they contain or the herbs I add. I don't really want to cook vegetables with two variations of doneness, yet her pearly whites no longer chew through fibrous foods. The same goes for her morning grapefruit and most red meats. All highly processed stuff goes down smoothly: cakes and coffee cakes, cookies, crackers, white bread, mashed and baked potatoes, squash, avocados, yams.

I now resort to lovely jars of artichoke salad, pickled Italian vegetables, three bean combinations, all foods that she will eat, so we're learning to do the same. We three are big on sweets but rather than baking chocolate chip cookies weekly like I used to, I've been relying on packaged treats by Pepperidge Farms and Nob Hill, and Bundt cakes from Raley's supermarket. Damn the cholesterol torpedoes, my new attitude is: Any prepared food in a storm.

↔

It's hard to believe that Momma remains ambulatory. We would not have known the odds against it except that at one point some medical folks described anticipating her arrival in a wheelchair; that's what her scans suggested. Nothing doing. At that point she was going to and fro at the helm of her four-wheeled walker. Then she fell while stepping into her garage.

The ER found no damage but two months later she could not get out of bed for the pain. New scans located a fracture that had gone previously undetected. A lengthy clinical description of her spinal deformations came home with us. It may have been a nurse who leaned in close and whispered, "Don't tell her all the stuff that's wrong with her back. If she knew, it might keep her from getting around."

Until she was 85, Momma sometimes wore shoes with a two-inch heel. At that age she fell at home, fracturing her foot (wearing flats, not heels). That's when we retrofitted her house with grab bars and railings, and that's when we found new homes for most of the extraneous garments that were hanging from doorknobs, the tops of doors, and along the handrails of the unused treadmill in her spare bedroom. There was simply too much stuff for an unsteady person to push past. Momma always said she was extra careful while navigating her home and yard, but, of course, home is where all her falls took place.

I suspect two things have kept Momma going: 1) Pickle Dog, acquired from the humane society a little more than nine years ago; and, 2) Her sense of invincibility. Same as the rest of us, she probably expected to live better and/or longer than her parents and in-laws, feeling younger than her years. When she moved to Nevada she had already survived the Great Depression, the loss of an infant child and the decline of a first marriage. Remarried, she persevered through her second husband's wartime service and his subsequent lethal heart attack, which transformed her into a single mother raising a teenage son.

She recounts how some local man tried to squeeze her out of her deceased husband's insurance business, offering her a pittance for it while trying to convince her that owning a business was no job for a woman. She didn't fall for his ruse. She ran the business for some time before selling it to a reputable buyer. Of course others have weathered as much, or more, the slow cascade of bad luck arriving just in time to offset one's sense that health and happiness stand at the door, fists upraised to knock.

Momma must have felt the same invincibility that makes me hopeful about physically faring better than my mother. I'll have paid more attention to nutrition and exercise and will benefit from advances in medical technology. And yet, from what I can tell, decline is inevitable, like that drunk driver who twenty-five years ago hydroplaned into my lane on a rainy winter night.

I braked hard, my brain instantaneously recognizing that the sheltered overpass offered no escape, nor did the oncoming traffic lane.

I made choices during that crash but could not avoid the long-term physical consequences accreting since then. For years afterwards I wished I could travel back in time just long enough to slap that driver really hard. But, no such magic. No reversing what the world sets into motion through others' choices or my own. Will I fare better than my elders? Not necessarily. It's more likely that I will simply fare differently.

I can name that bird in three beats

The casting call for my imaginary post-golden years consists mainly of yard birds—the scrub jays, robins, sparrows, and mourning doves which frequent our backyard feeders and scavenge the seeds I scatter for them.

I can picture sitting for hours, studying the passage of seasons with only the changing of the bloom-guards to mark the days: a handful of crocus delicately cupping winter's last breath, twelve narcissus pushing skyward. Over there, the lush pink of a dwarf nectarine tree, followed by bee balm, lavatera, autumn sedum, fall crocus, each blooming in succession.

A bonus will be the winged migrants who appear for a deep drink from the repurposed dog bowl: red-eyed towhees and a flock or two of Cedar waxwings drawn to such crab-apples as remain.

I might try to channel that *Peanuts* comic strip character who pats birds on the head. I always did like him. Or, maybe I should take up working crossword puzzles. A puzzle moves slowly, perhaps just my speed.

There. I'm making plans already.

↔

October ~

Preparations for a medical appointment. Momma doesn't go out "without her face on," so today I played cosmetician. Macular degeneration has robbed the detail from her central vision and altered the colors of things. To her, orange looks pink and almost anything of medium tone looks white.

I've got the making-up process down to a few minutes—foundation, eyebrow pencil, lipstick, a bit of blusher on the apples of her cheeks.

Me: You look elegant.

Momma: I used to be elegant sometimes, but now it's not much for me.

Years ago, when she lived in her own home, we arrived to transport her to meet her best friend for dinner at a local restaurant. She came to the door and at first I wasn't sure what looked wrong. Then I caught on. She had penciled her eyebrows with her forest green eyeliner. What to do? I thought she might want to wipe them clean and use a gray pencil instead, but no. When I asked if she knew she'd used her green pencil, she said, "I meant to. I thought it was a nice color."

Off we went. I suppose some people who saw her that evening noticed her interesting choice, and some of them may have thought us remiss in our duties by letting an elder go out in public like that. But it wasn't as if the restaurant would refuse to serve her; her money spent as well as anyone else's.

Momma may take after her aunt Ennie, who knew what she liked. She liked a pink house. Perhaps her choice would have proven relatively tame until applied to the entire exterior of what is commonly painted a neutral color. Her neighborhood was full of tan and gray houses, a brown here and a pale green there. Not Ennie's. I can imagine someone directing the firemen to her home: "Don't know the exact address, but turn onto 15th and you can't miss it."

Pink made Ennie happy, and that's what mattered. When we packed her personal effects to move her closer to us, every dress in her closet was pink. Every single one.

Anyway, after Momma moved into our home I disposed of her green eyeliner pencil, and a blue one I found in her makeup stash. You know, just in case.

↔

Sometimes, after visiting our mother my eldest brother debriefs with me. After years of hearing how she missed the raised garden beds he had built for her in California, he built two in the yard of her current home. She went with him to buy the supplies and kept his ice water replenished as he worked on them.

When I visited her later, she said, "Your brother wanted them. I didn't really want them but he insisted. There was no good place for them and now they're hard to mow around."

That's one of a steady stream of dissatisfactions she spends time enumerating: faulty home-improvement projects, the declining quality of restaurant food and wait-staff, poor service by retail clerks, the selection of supermarket products, stormy weather, the behavior of elected officials, the long wait time for free tax advice, the attitudes of people playing cards at the senior center ... I could go on.

This always makes me wonder where such a perspective comes from. Long years as a lone head of household? A need to control her environment and the people in her space? I wish I knew because I'm trying to devise a strategy for dealing with the negativity. I mean, instead of skipping my next visit.

↔

November ~

Presidential candidate Herman Cain has been in the TV news and the subject of newspaper accounts. Momma, still a southerner at heart, carries racial attitudes from down the years that can show up without warning.

Today she said something about how she couldn't imagine people voting for "that man." A person might have assumed she was shocked and disappointed by his admitted infidelities, but we know she doesn't any longer assimilate the details of news stories, can't process information the way she once could.

Jim asked her: Why, because he's black? You voted for Obama. He is too.

Momma: Well, he looks white to me.

That and the fact that he wasn't G.W. Bush had assured her vote. Perhaps as our aging population develops macular degeneration, more candidates of color will get elected to public office. How's that for a silver lining?

When Momma first came to live with us we had an aide named Liz, a gregarious hardworking sort, cheerful, and impervious to upset. She was a transplant to our city from California, which is nothing if not ethnically and racially diverse.

One day I came home from errands to hear that Momma had used the N-word while relating an anecdote to Liz. In the past I had described her racist terms as wrong. I had also gently corrected her use of negro, nigra, and colored. My husband had even corrected her during a visit to a doctor's office.

This time I got mad. I planted my hands on the arms of her wheelchair and leaned so close that we almost touched noses. I told her that we don't talk like that in this house and that I knew she was smarter than that, that I expected she was capable of a better vocabulary.

Later I realized that those were the first truly harsh words I have expressed to her in our decades as family, and I hope they're the last.

↔

November 18 ~

When she noticed me standing alongside her bed, Momma said: Have you always been an early riser?

I had already let Pickle Dog out and back in, and emptied the commode bucket. I said: No. You were ringing your bell and it woke me and I came in to see what you need.

Momma: Oh. Then you can go back to bed.

Such an innocent-looking object

I washed my hands and crawled in beside my husband, who had already been up twice with our big dog. That's how our predawn mornings go these days: pee break, dog break, Pickle break, then the furnace comes on and I have to shove the covers off. In short, my sleep is never solid.

In other news: A house far south of us caught fire overnight. Rising winds turned embers and flames into an inferno that burned hundreds of acres and destroyed more than twenty homes and buildings. Hundreds were evacuated. At the Riley homestead we have little worth complaining about.

↔

Thanksgiving ~

Enjoyed a lovely dinner at the home of Jim's cousin and her husband. As always, good company and delicious food. Because it's an effort for Momma to navigate their front stoop plus the steps up and down to and from the living room and dining room, we took her wheelchair. Their guest bathroom has no grab bars or toilet rails and her wheelchair just barely fits in, but when we are there we manage. Two people and one rolling chair fit in with the door closed.

My mother used to describe her father as a voyeur because her parents left the door open when using their bathroom and Grandpa would sometimes stroll past when Grandma was busy there. Mother thought her father liked to see her mother with her pants down.

As a person who lived alone, Momma left the bathroom door open when on the throne, and we do the same if we leave her unattended. That's because if she falls and comes to rest against the closed door there will be no way to get the door open with her weight against it and no way to unhinge it from the hall. We (or the EMTs) would have to remove the entire bathroom window to accomplish the rescue.

Of course, Grandpa may have been a randy old soul. He was a bit of a lady's man in his younger years.

↔

November 27 ~

Momma fell in the living room tonight, narrowly missing the burled-wood coffee table and banging hard against an upholstered loveseat arm. She meant to look for her nasal inhaler among the cushions behind her, but lost her balance and tumbled forward. Though she weighs only 120 pounds or so, it took two of us to lift her. The fall—more of a collapse—had knocked the air out of her.

Shortly thereafter she joined us for dinner, but ended up retiring to bed early. We've been daily applying Lidoderm patches to her spine to ease her discomfort. Now we applied one to the sorest spot on her ribcage and reminded her to ring the bell for assistance during the night. In her pajama pocket we found the "sniffer" she'd been looking for when she fell.

↔

November 28 ~

This was to be my day off from the house, but we spent the morning preparing Momma for a trip to the emergency room to have the pain in her ribcage assessed.

The EMTs were terrific, gentle but direct. They conducted a non-emergency transport because we couldn't fold Momma into my car for the ride. For some reason, the ER was barely busy; must have been the post-holiday effect. Our time there spanned only four hours.

The ER doc was one we'd seen before. After "taking pictures," as Momma calls it, he diagnosed a bruised rib, or at least not a fracture, which they wouldn't treat anyway. She had sustained the natural consequence of falling against an immoveable object. He recommended she sleep on the injured side to allow the non-injured side to expand and contract with her breathing.

The doc could not prescribe strong meds for Momma's bruised rib because when she last took a combination of pain drugs plus antibiotics for a touch of bronchitis, there were unintended effects. After two or three days of taking those prescriptions, she spent the night talking to a handful of people hovering above her bed, somehow at ceiling height.

Various characters visited her during the night, some of whom she recognized from her days as Worthy Grand Matron of the Order of the Eastern Star. Others wore uniforms and might have been police or sheriff officers. One sad lady seemed to be trying to "stay inside the building" while Momma and others were locking up, and Momma was worried that she needed a ride home.

We took turns assuring her that no strangers were on her bedroom ceiling and no one was trying to take her little dog. The next day we delivered her to the hospital and they weaned her off the meds.

This time around we are sticking with Tylenol.

↔

November 29 ~

Help arrived in the form of a personal aide and I got to meet with an arborist for a discussion about how to water our trees during the winter drought our area is suffering. At 11:00 a.m. I went to the movie theater to catch My Week with Marilyn, followed by a lunch of muffaletta sandwich made with pesto, followed by shopping for Christmas gifts for Momma's nieces, and then forty-five minutes of writing at Bibo, a local café.

Got home in time to help with dinner, then dusted the house and wrapped gifts.

Jim looked up from his book and said: It's your day off. Oh, there aren't any days off, are there?

I was going to scrub the toilets but my energy gave out and I sat for twenty minutes in front of a television rerun of Storage Wars before helping Momma prepare for bed. She agreed that she may need to ring for help in the night, so I tied a second one to the far bedrail.

The Rat growled and snapped at me as I attached bell number two. Momma put out her hand to quiet her little love and received the same disrespect.

I wrapped a hot, damp towel around my shoulders and went to bed to read.

↔

December 1 ~

We have rearranged the living room furniture to make a path for Momma to walk indoor circuits for exercise. Anyone who visits will wonder why the coffee table is shoved up against the sofa, but with a little advance notice we can set it in order and they'll never have to guess.

↔

December 5 ~
Our schedule of last night:
9:00 p.m. Momma to bed; after finishing chores we read in bed
11:00 p.m. Lights out
1:45 a.m. Momma rang the bell for help using her commode
3:00 a.m. Big dog needed to go out
6:00 a.m. Jim's alarm went off; he got up to prepare for hunting
7:00 a.m. Jim woke me for a kiss goodbye; left with his dog

7:30 a.m. Momma rang the bell; Psycho Dog needed to go out
8:30 a.m. I rose to get the household under way

You know how Presidents appear to age during their years in office? I figure presidential years equate roughly to dog years. Tending years have similar dimensions through time and space. I'm still trying to calculate how many extra years I've aged while Tending.

↔

December 6 ~

Bought dark brown winter shoes for Momma. She always says no to brown, but she will think these are black. The clerk told me that another woman had come in recently to buy shoes for her 103-year-old mother, who "puts herself together" every day and goes out for lunch with friends and to play bridge. One hundred-three … in our situation that would mean six more years of multiple nighttime interruptions. Hmm.

I fetched Chinese takeout for dinner, one of Momma's favorites, except when it's not. Then I went to a meeting with writer friends. When I returned, I asked Momma how she had liked her dinner.

Momma: It wasn't as good as the last time.

Me: I thought you said it was okay last time.

Momma: That last time wasn't as good as the time before and this time was less good than the last time.

I sampled some of the sweet and sour and a bit of the won ton soup. It tasted fine to me. Later I mentioned Momma's displeasure to my husband, who'd been home with her for dinner. He said she'd had seconds.

↔

Winter activities ~

One of Jim's cousins came by for a visit. Momma's nieces, both petite beauties, regularly visit their auntie. Their mother died years ago and Momma is one of only two siblings left from the original seven; her surviving younger sister lives in New York. Each cousin stops by about once a month, usually on a Sunday after church.

For a two-year span during high school, the cousins lived with Momma and Jim because their mother had moved away with her new husband. Momma was a widow with a son at home, but she accommodated both girls so that they could stay together and the youngest could graduate with her classmates. I've always thought that speaks to Momma's generosity.

As this niece took her leave she said to Momma, "I love you." For once, Momma, who is notoriously undemonstrative, replied in kind. When we got to the front door, Jim's cousin pumped her fist in victory. "I got an 'I love you'," she exclaimed. "I'm going to call my sis and rub it in!"

We later heard she'd done just that.

↔

My father died young enough that I never watched him grow old. I like to think I would have dealt fine with an elder version of him as he was a congenial type and might not have turned sour. As it was, he drank himself to death, which was a slow and sloppy way to go.

Alcohol was a taste he acquired in his early-middle years. It started with a beer or two after mowing the lawn or while dipping a line over the side of Gramps' aluminum fishing boat. A cold brew on a hot summer day must have tasted like nectar, but it was probably his gateway drug, leading him to martinis, Rusty Nails, and other exotic lubricants.

Dad was reticent, which made him seem cerebral, but clearly his brainpower could not regulate his unhealthy habit. After my parents decamped from their marriage his alcoholism became a great white whale.

My mother went to a newly independent life and he to a marriage wherein his new wife (an old friend) poured him drinks on request, sometimes starting at noon. We never called her our step-mother; she was simply "his wife." She bought a bar in downtown Sacramento where, misery loving company, he would sometimes spend an afternoon or evening. I always considered her accomplice to his death.

Dad had been arrested more than once for driving under the influence and had spent time at a rehab clinic in Yountville, California. His participation was probably court-ordered, though he never owned up to that aspect of it. In spite of such interventions his unnatural urges proved too strong. Or were they natural? And just when does substance use cross the line from whim or fancy to something as necessary as breathing?

One night, alone at home, he died. No last phone calls, no goodbyes. We missed out on his being a grandfather to our family, a wise guy, a sharer of stories. Instead, he was gone with much left unsaid.

↔

More of the Tolerable Bits
Multiple bathroom breaks, sometimes hourly
Hallucinations caused by meds
Providing manicures and pedicures
Partially chewed food left on the plate
Doorjambs banged up by wheelchair and cane
Making wardrobe repairs
The constant low-volume humming,
    gasps, farts, and grunts
Working in my bedroom for the quiet of it

Things That Make Me Grumpy
Sleep hours interrupted for a deranged dog
Pets on the furniture, shedding like mad
Being treated like a waitress
Uncovered sneezes

↔

At some point this last year I read an account by Patti Davis, the daughter of President Ronald Reagan and Nancy Reagan. The former First Lady is now a frail, hard-to-please widow. Patti describes high and low points, how she tries to please her mother without being run over by her, feeling like a thirteen-year-old in the process. Can you imagine? The daughter of a former First Lady flinching under her mother's disapproving gaze. I experienced a twinge of envy that she feels thirteen while I've been known to feel twelve. It seems that even the rich and famous can suffer an ordinary disconnect. When I read Patti's account I thought, *Jesus*, even a former First Lady is reduced to her basic disappointments.

↔

December 17 ~

Since an aide was scheduled for a longer shift, I took a drive north and west, out through northern California's Sierra Valley.

The wind was vigorous, not enough to rock the car, but just right for scrubbing the sky clean of the haze that's been hanging around lately. A nice day for a walk, but even better for a drive.

I like almost nothing better than to saddle up my car and drive out of the city. It's not far before housing developments give way to burnished hills of sage and rabbit brush abutting strings of slate-blue mountains, which would be snowbound were this a normal year. (We're two months into winter with no precipitation, what's that about?) I hate to think of drought as the new normal and I will be mightily displeased to ever give up showers or ration how often I flush the toilet.

↔

CJ called today. Her stepchildren, JN's kids, won't be making it to a holiday dinner they were trying to plan. She lamented, "It'll just be old people." By that she meant they'd have to do without the grown kids and the one grandchild. Just her and JN and his brothers and father. I had to laugh. We're the same generation, she and I, and she had confirmed it: We're all old people now.

↔

Dear Dad,

I think you would have liked the dictionaries I seem to acquire these days. A woman friend of mine plans to "win" by dying with the most jewelry, but I like old books, though I am particular about which ones I adopt. I favor dictionaries and thesauri and various reference books of eras past. Perhaps when I bought Jim a two-book set about the YMCA's involvement in troop comfort during WWI, the volumes were actually for me. When he reads this he might think, Hey!

I don't recall you as a reader of books. Music, though, that was your thing—big band, a little jazz, some easy listening stuff. Last month I bought a double disc set of a 1950s recording of Bill Evans, an accomplished jazz pianist. His versions of My Funny Valentine and Alfie transport me backwards through time. See? I have learned to appreciate the roots of the rock music you disdained.

I have a few of your letters and written works. They were Mother's treasures, I'm sure, even if they reminded her of promises poorly kept or else abandoned. It was through your letters and writings that I came to know you as someone other than that somber figure who came home from work to a noisy brood. You never spoke about dreams or desires. No such sharing.

For as much as you were a man of your times, you might have been happier in the twenty-first century, the better to write, to publish, and to cry when needed. Perhaps instead of making a family you would have fashioned a life as a foreign correspondent, a troubadour, a shooting star.

I don't expect to meet you in an afterlife. You would not have believed in one either, so I'll say it to the sky and the warm Nevada wind: I wanted healthier, happier end-years for you. I wanted more for you, and more for me within the more for you. I am now the age you were when you died like someone old. You make me want my remaining years to count for something.

Recently, three of us went to that place on Jamison Creek where long ago we spread your ashes. I snapped a few photos of the downstream turn where the dust of you once disappeared around the bend, but none of them did the place justice. My favorites from that afternoon turned out to be the close-ups of riffling water at my feet, pebbles and rocks like smooth round changelings peering skyward through the summer shallows.

As I write this, I am sitting in the pale sun of a summer day on the California coast, the fog and pounding surf holding echoes of your youth. Your chosen escape, though, would have been a day of fly fishing on a mountain stream; the whip of line through air dense with aromas of growth and decay; the birdsong of nuthatches from a nearby Jeffrey pine; and the constant, watery motion mirroring time running out before you.

That kind of place would have felt like an antidote to life's ordinary troubles. It would have felt like heaven.

↔

Back at Thanksgiving time Momma had mentioned that since one of her two nieces has non-pierced ears, that niece should come for first dibs on pieces in Momma's jewelry collection. Eventually we worked out a schedule; first one then the other came for visits during which we pulled out multiple drawers of sparkling brooches, earrings, necklaces, bracelets.

In the 1940s, 50s, and 60s, Momma dressed the way women did then---wearing hats and gloves, matching brooches and earrings, perhaps matching handbags. She says it felt good to dress up. Those were also the days of gentlemen (business men especially) wearing fedoras as they boarded trains and carpools. To spy such fully-dressed people these days you'd have to frequent the uptown district of a large metropolitan city, or people-watch on the opera house steps.

So many pretties, and so few places to wear them

In the twenty-five years I've known Jim's mother, not only have fashions changed, but Momma's choices have grown a bit less formal. She favors slacks and untucked blouses, earrings that don't pinch, and rings that fit over her swollen knuckles. She has by necessity simplified her adornment.

Maybe her jewelry collection represented the *good* years, the decades of work and socializing and travel, reconstituted by memory with a glance at gems and strands and things that pin on. Every so often she requests that we pull out the various drawers containing her holdings. As she lifts pieces out she recalls some of the stories behind certain pieces and how they came into her possession. Others? Well, they are pretty, but no longer aligned with special outfits or occasions. She might say, "I don't know how that got here."

Much of her costume jewelry is good quality, middle-class relatives of richer, finer jewelry. Little of it would suit our daughter, though I suspect she would be glad for Momma to offer. It's my intent that if she wants to she'll shop the collection … some day.

As it was, each of Momma's nieces carried home three dozen pieces and there were still dozens left. We had previously put aside Momma's few favorites, the ones she thought she might wear again someday (though of course she will not), and then it turned out we had forgotten to "shop" through her necklaces. Ah well, something for another day.

↔

December 20 ~

Our daughter arrived back in town recently for a break from grad school. She has a condo that is too small for the hosting of holiday gatherings (plus, I imagine she would rather not), so once again we will take charge.

Our holidays are not all airy and light, in part because there seems to be an insurmountable barrier between our daughter and Momma. It's that problem of children being vulnerable to a relative's insensitivity. There must be people who are not affected by how family members speak to them, but that's not anyone I know. Same old story: It's the people we care about who can hurt us.

Momma had raised a son but never a daughter, and wasn't much involved in her granddaughter's childhood, in part due to her disconnect with Jim's first wife. I can picture our daughter's mother as diffident, even dismissive, toward Momma. Perhaps it was mutual.

Our daughter is forty and during a long run with our county's Public Guardian's office dealt with all manner of indigent, infirm, and elderly people. She knows her way around old people, cranky people, demented people, and adults who have been abused and neglected. Her extensive experience provides little armor. Momma can speak across the great divide of years and sting her with a very few words. I wish it were different, but it's not.

Just this visit, though, something may have shifted when our daughter witnessed her grandmother in action with my husband and others. She may have noted Momma's memory troubles and continuing physical decline.

The meal was long over and conversations at the table and elsewhere in the room were waning. For a minute our daughter stood beside me in the kitchen. "You know," she said, motioning toward the family room where Momma sat watching television. "You're taking care of this end of things. If you need me to check on your mom, just let me know. It wouldn't trouble me at all."

At first I drew a blank and then a synapse fired. Momma's sometimes harsh words don't faze me; I can brush them off. My own mother's words though ... a whole other story. Our daughter was right—she and I are each immune to the other's elder.

Jim explained to me later that our daughter had heard about Momma's call to her diabetic, overweight sister. The second sentence out of Momma's mouth had been, "Did you see about that fat pill on TV? ... (a pause while she listened) ... That *fat pill*."

No doubt her sister took Momma's query in stride. They've been communicating for almost ninety years and are the last of their generation. Notwithstanding Momma's references to fat pills and fat in general, they're probably solidly in each other's camp (though there may be times when they give thanks for living at opposite ends of the country).

Today I was relating some of the above details to Sherry, my hair stylist of 25+ years when it came to me: What if there was such a thing as elder swapping? Not a social network, but a social services network linking elders with Tenders in a way that allows one person to switch their attention to someone else's elder while taking a break from the craziness of their own family. Like the way produce co-ops provide fresh fruits and veggies to subscribers, each participant receiving a share.

Or maybe I'm describing a barter system, with Tenders trading just the social parts of the deal. It could include the exchange of visits and perhaps even simple errands: a half-hour visit to someone in long-term care, a delivery of cookies or an African violet, a willing ear for the recitation of stories that haven't yet grown stale for the listener. Mother, father, or spouse gets to complain or reminisce or dish about family or lost loves. Criticism rolls off like rainwater. Elders would enjoy more variety in their lives, and Tenders would benefit from a change of duty. Of course I haven't worked out all the kinks, like safety protocols or background checks, but I like the premise.

I know, I know. *Ideally,* we so deeply love our elders and other needy kin that we weather every disability, proclivity, mean streak, etc., without succumbing to the emotional fatigue waiting for its cue to step on stage. We expect to channel Ozzie and Harriet. Oh, wait—they're fiction.

Under the influence of hot air — a BIG IDEA

Not up for swapping? Home health agencies can provide companions. One of my friends has made that type of arrangement for her mother, who resides in an assisted living facility. The mother's companion takes her to the store to buy snacks, watches television with her, and converses, all the while assessing the mother's functioning.

The aides who come daily to our house act as companions and hands-on helpers. There's a lot of visiting about children, weather, national news stories, and all manner of small talk. They act as surrogates for Jim and me. Otherwise we just might need to organize a co-op.

↔

Another New Year's Day arrives ~

We slept in after an evening of takeout chicken dinner shared with two longtime family friends. Jim teamed with Carl, and I teamed with Claudia for a series of pinochle card games. That's how we always do it—husbands versus wives. This time the men won handily, but had the good sense not to gloat too much.

Jim and Carl have been buddies since their university days, and then through Army basic training. They have a story about getting a tank so mired in mud that it had to be abandoned and another about finding a rubber tarantula under a bed and thinking it was real. Memories they wouldn't trade for money.

As midnight ticked closer, the men began to play table football. One thing led to another, all of us bleary-eyed, when Carl began pantomiming Jim in a way that reduced us to hysterics. The kind of hiccupping laughter that cramps your stomach, where breaths turn into snorts and your sight turns blurry. When midnight struck, we were so spent we had to call it quits. Somehow I suspect we contain reserves of laughter and tears to be shared another time.

We crawled out of bed at 9:00 this morning after 6:00 and 7:30 a.m. dog wake-up calls. Later, Psycho Dog tried to bite me when I reached for the newspaper that Momma motioned me to take from her.

Me: I should snap her on the nose.

Momma: No. Don't snap her on the nose. That's the problem.

I wanted to say, "The problem is you are at the table with a decrepit dog that's been taught that she's a person, one of the bosses, instead of one of the dogs."

But I didn't. Instead, I went for a walk, a strategy I use for self-directed time outs.

After dinner, the CBS magazine show 60 Minutes came on. One segment told about a young man who took SAT tests for high school students in exchange for cash. Next up, a commercial for a compilation of Andy Rooney segments (Rooney's shtick was as a curmudgeon, or maybe that was the *real* Rooney). The commercial showed quick cuts of the young Andy and the old Andy. In one he said something like, "I hate to deal with finances."

Momma looked over at me and said: There are a lot of employers who wouldn't want to hear that from someone.

First I tried recalling which employers had been mentioned in the SAT story. None.

Then I said: Those students are in college now, so they might not even be working. That guy was taking tests for them when they were in high school.

Momma: Big companies can send people to school to learn about money.

(At last I understood) Me: *That* was a commercial for stories from 60 Minutes. Andy Rooney was grousing about stuff he didn't like. He was known for that—grousing.

Momma: Oh.

Life must appear stranger and stranger when everything around you is speeding up while your internal processes are slowing down.

↔

Dear Nieces o'Mine,

Here is what I think of when I picture you girls journeying through summers past to visit us for a week of exuberant, youthful escape from home: My eyes drank you in, your smooth summer skin, your slant of nose, how fast-grown you seemed since the last time. The youngest one's waterfall of inky hair, the middle one's pale fan of blond. And big sister's coloring a blend of both.

Do you remember our travels in my car, headed here and there and back again, the spelling quizzes directed from my command post at the wheel, and my cautions about boyfriends, sex, and drugs? We have all traveled beyond an auntie's monologues.

You know how I rarely keep my distance. If you stand near I will reach for a shoulder, a waist, a hug. Timing is of no consequence—

sleepy-eyed mornings, during dinner preparations, or your trajectory toward bed—fair game, all. My weathered hands reach out, telegraphing nonsense and other love to receptive, yielding girl-women. Once our holiday meals are reduced to bones, the car repairs set to rights, the sister-fights negotiated and dismissed, I hope you remember this about me: I reach for you.

↔

Mid-January starts our third year as Tenders ~

We were at the table tonight with network news on across the room, behind Momma's back, actually, since her dinner place faces away from the family room. The coverage was about Martin Luther King Jr. Day, with video clips of his "I Have a Dream" speech.

Momma: So what is it that Martin Luther King is trying to accomplish?

Jim: He's not here anymore, but he led civil rights protests and today is the holiday in his honor.

Momma: I thought they took care of all that.

Jim and I looked at each other. I suppose we were both wondering how to interpret her remark.

Jim asked: Took care of what?

Momma: All that stuff.

Me: He's been dead for almost fifty years, so this is the day that honors him.

Momma: For what?

Me: For fighting for equal rights for black Americans.

Momma: Didn't they shoot him?

Jim: He was assassinated back in the 60s.

Momma: Oh. That's what I thought.

↔

January 24 ~

Today I watched a PBS special about Johannesburg, South Africa, and the civil rights struggle by black South Africans against apartheid. Nelson Mandela and a man named Tomba, and others. Momma wanted to know what I'd been watching, so I explained that it was about the black struggle for equality.

Momma: Well, I don't believe all people are equal.

Ellen, who is Native American, sat up a fraction straighter.

I tried to express my opinion that though we are not all the same, in this case equality means equal opportunities for all. I got a nod from Momma but no answer. Sometimes it's like she hasn't left the South of her youth. Other times she's curious about Indian issues and asks questions that suggests a person respectful of all ethnicities and cultures.

As for equality, I guess we will all be equal once we are old. There will be presidents and people of power or intellect who will soil their pants. Supermodels and geniuses will become everyman, and the cancer of learned authors will turn lethal. Age and infirmities will stand front and center as the great equalizers.

↔

What I Meant to Say ~

Shirley died of cancer almost four years ago. No one else fills the space she left behind, but lessons learned through her persist because it's impossible not to carry them along like particles of sunshine caught in my pores. I recall sitting in her hospice room making small talk, wondering how a person arrives at such an end with grace. Those bits of her journey could have been yesterday.

At some point the anvil drops and you realize time is running out. All the years you thought lay ahead compact themselves into just a few weeks, like cars accordioned on the freeway. Maybe what remains are mere months, or hours, and not many at that. Time that once seemed adequate for your needs is apparently a mere drop, less than other people will spend rushing to meet sales quotas or watching TV shows parsed from laugh tracks.

For you, though, life itself is reduced to the newly important—lungs expanding to capture the universe, then an exhalation to make room for another sip of hydrogen and its friend oxygen. And then, if you're lucky, one more.

Speaking about Shirley's particular cancer, her doctor said, "We've done all we can. We're out of treatment options. Plan on a week, maybe two … depending. Cancer multiplies rapidly; it's everywhere."

That's when I thought of all the things a person leaves unsaid.

The things you think you have a lifetime to convey. For instance, I meant to tell my nieces what others may not have told them, what their parents probably have not. I wanted them to hear, "You will be okay. These seem like tough times. You're trying to find yourself, trying to figure out how much to let go and how hard to hold on. You might be calculating which friends are keepers and which you can live without. They're just practice, pop quizzes, so don't worry about getting them exactly right; you have decades ahead." I would have added, "You feel you have to rush. It's natural. Young people hurry to reach the next hour, the next day, to see what's coming and to discover who will surprise them and what will make their hearts thump. But don't worry about what you're missing. There's no capturing it all. Just observe the world churning around you and examine the bits that stick in your head. Be mindful and happy and young while you can. The larger world will bear down soon enough."

Remembering Shirley makes me ponder the handful of friends who might leap to my defense and how I regret not having created more reasons for such leaps. Inside I'm a wooly sort, but all these years I've been licking my palm and smoothing down the sticking-out parts. Reluctant conformist, sporadic pisser-and-moaner, but not too loud. Few know my dark center, the cranky-pants-at-midnight-when-the-dog-is-barking me. Is it too late to reveal more of those traits? When does it become too late?

One day Shirley said, "What doesn't kill you makes you stronger." That same week her doctor explained, "We have good medicine for the pain. There's no reason for unrelenting pain. When regular doses aren't enough, we use fast-acting meds under the tongue."

I nodded my head and imagined the feel of drops against gums and teeth. How a liquid peace would wash through flesh and bones to quiet the pain while blood still throbbed through tissues and organs, feeding a cancer that has spread its picnic blanket and settled in to stay.

The drugs allow a lovely drift among the clouds of a person's mind. One minute you're talking to someone who looks familiar and knows your name, the next you think she's the nurse aide. Why hasn't she put your untouched milk away for later? "Oh, I see now, she's not staff."

Speaking of the familiar, I am grateful for a particular friendship founded way back in 1970. Seventh grade brought a summer of sun-warmed pavement and 45 rpm records on the turntable. We danced and sang, and tested curfews, and at least once a week I raced home from her house to arrive late for dinner.

I can still taste the hot summer air overlaid with my Emeraude cologne, a fragrance green and grassy. Her older brother kissed me. She kissed me too, just once, to see if there were any sparks, but no. How many years ago was that? Roughly forty-three, but who's counting.

I used to think that when I got to the end I'd be gracious about how many years I'd lived, but now I'm not so sure. Now I'm inclined to think I might wail and gnash my teeth and make a fuss just because it's allowed when you're dying. Rules change and bets get cancelled. Misbehavior and poor manners and confusion and anger—all of it allowed, encouraged even, because so much else is beyond your control. When you get to the end you don't steer the ship anymore. Almost everyone else does, but not you.

I wonder now ... when *my* last day comes, who will empty my refrigerator one last time so that no food spoils? I can't stand to waste perfectly good food when in my own city there are people going hungry. Children even. I suppose a young friend or two will handle the dirty work, emptying closets and watering plants. She'll find my dog a new home and he'll cancel the mail. I hope they turn out to be people I've treated well so that the giving and receiving even out. No such thing as perfection, but wouldn't it be nice for the scales to approximately balance at the closing bell?

For a while I worked for our county, which had a policy of allowing employees to transfer unused vacation time to others during emergencies. Issued from one friend on behalf of another, an e-mail would arrive calling for donations of time. The payroll office accepted contributions in one-week increments, nothing less. Soon the person facing tough times, say a child's recovery from surgery, would have five or six weeks of paid leave. As donation maxed out, the air around our desks grew thick with the department's collective sigh of relief.

This set me to thinking. What if life itself worked that way? Someone down the hall in the Life Accounting Department could request a week or a month from those destined for a long life for transferring to someone whose alarm is set to go off in the wee hours. Think about how much time would pour in! People would rationalize, "What's a week in the scope of things? I can afford that much." Even strangers might donate for that uptick of warmth at a good deed done.

Before needing those quick-acting meds you'd want to use your donated time for another walk along the lakeshore, or to take in one more action film, or to spin tales over a lunch of Pad Thai. You know, before you hit the slippery patch.

Best use your bonus promptly because this is your brain on cancer+morphine: You might tell a visiting friend, "You all have made a big mess of this," or describe the bustling Filipina who just now put you to bed in clean nightclothes as "one tough Jewish mama."

Hallucinations too. You fall into the framed floral print bolted to the wall, Alice down the rabbit hole. Swimming back to the surface leaves you breathless. And questions get lost in space before you can voice them, becoming fractured observations sporting leftover punctuation.

Life segues into dreams pinched between moments of wakefulness: that March sojourn to Death Valley when a million flowers bloomed like sun bubbling up from the desert floor; two tiny dogs asleep on your chest that vanish as your eyelids open. Never again the squeak-slam of the front screen door, never the pungent tang of sagebrush after a sudden squall, or the mountain patchwork of balsamroot and desert peach, wild grasses and sego lilies. Never again Tahoe's blue dazzle to break your heart, just this glow of fluorescent lights down a bone-pale corridor. You look beyond the linoleum floors and wilted flowers, the adjustable bed and the bolted window, and say to the woman sitting in the room's one armchair, "Tell me again ... just what hotel is this?"

On the bright side, every story, each warped directive, invective, or backwards memory trades at face value. No intent to deceive, no purposeful evasion. No one need protest.

At one point, Shirley questioned whether the clock had run out for examining her life. I asked her but she couldn't explain just how she might have fallen short of some personal ideal. The details eluded her. A faraway look in her eyes told me she was right then contemplating the moments she could recall as well-lived, or faith-filled, or just plain fine, and maybe a few other times when she'd strayed a little from the path she was on. And so I said a prayer that she find peace within her contemplations because it seems that at some point a person must quit worrying.

I know that the closer to dying or watching someone die, the more some people fret. But as far as I can tell, being upset doesn't fix anything. I told Shirley that from my vantage point she had acquitted herself with dignity; might as well take a nap.

I recently read a book that contained advice about living, about observing the swirl around us while remaining present in the moment. It recommended that we live like we are dying. At first I thought the notion profound, and then I realized—well, we *are*.

Which brings me back to what I was thinking at the onset: To my family, TK, TKK, JoMi, and others of my inner circle, plus a handful of folks in the larger universe, like that nice lady at the bakery and the kid with the goofy grin who bags groceries ... I want to say something before it's too late. I will miss you someday. Someday I will be missing you.

↔

January 29 ~

Caught a movie today with my husband, making the third or fourth time in the last year+ that we've been out together. Our normal routine is a sharing of duties, reminiscent of couples in this gaming town of ours who work split shifts—for instance, one person working day shift while the other works swing (afternoon to evening). Because casinos, some of our largest employers, operate 24-hours a day, many spouses and roommates end up with offset shifts. It beats being unemployed and when you're young you can probably adapt to almost any schedule. It's hard on romance, though.

Jim and I are not young anymore, but we seem these days to pass like ships under a noon sky, one going out to run errands or have a bit of leisure, the other staying behind for tending. At least we both attempt sleep in the same bed. Together.

Today at the theater there were three ladies ahead of us buying tickets. It was 11:00 a.m. and Jim had given up his mid-morning dog walk to go with me.

Jim whispered: Oh my God. We're here with the little old ladies.
Me: Fops
Jim: Huh?
Me: Fops.

Jim: Oh, yeah.

You may have heard that term, which is the pronunciation for the acronym FOPs, but I had not before certain friends of ours used it one time while ferrying us around Yuma, Arizona. They spend their winter months luxuriating in the warmth of the Southwest amid many thousands of other snowbirds. Residents there often motor around in electric golf carts, and sometimes they drive their full-sized autos at the speed of a cart.

The FOP reference came from a man whose wife has assigned him the nickname Mister. Mister's warped sense of humor kicked in as we found ourselves behind someone cautiously navigating a Yuma street.

"Fop," he said, knowing we would look askance at him.

His explanation was deadpan. "Fucking old people," he said. "Fops." Our laughs welled up from deep inside because there we were visiting two seniors who sometimes drive their electric carts around Yuma. Mister gave us a sly look and a crooked smile. We had met the FOPs and they were us.

↔

A splendid February day ~

Today I attended a lecture by an Egyptologist, held at our local branch of the Osher Lifelong Learning Institute (OLLI). There a person may subscribe to classes and lectures and support groups once they turn 50. Members might not have yet reached their "golden years," but they're old enough to recognize how much they do not know and that they want to keep learning.

I gave my full attention to the speaker's observations and rationale, through his many slides of hieroglyphics and maps of archeological sites, until the last few minutes of his talk. At that point he proposed that aliens had assisted ancient Earthlings in their mathematical calculations, the construction of pyramids, and the smelting of a metal ingested by the wealthy to keep them strong and virile. That's when he lost me.

Still, the day's gifts were fulsome, having started with a city bowling tournament in the morning and continuing with a lunch downtown after the lecture. It didn't end there. After lunch, KH and I stepped across the street to the Riverside Theaters to see *The Iron*

Lady. Meryl Streep was an unstoppable force, convincing me that she *was* Margaret Thatcher through her tough middle years and into her decline.

I was home by 7:00 p.m. for leftovers from the dinner meal, cheffed up by *le husband*, who also tended his mother at bedtime. I watched a bit of television then read in bed. It felt like a whole day off, like virtually no other. Did I earlier call it splendid? That's the right word.

↔

Peg phoned in response to my voicemail message that said "You must be sick and tired of people asking you if you're sick and tired." We talked about her cancer, using the terminology orbiting her particular scenario: Stage IV, terminal, targeted drugs, genetic mutation. We also spoke about pleasanter concepts: how much she loves her work, her employee association projects, and the potential someday to travel around Nevada and beyond.

Judging by Peg's mien you'd be hard-pressed to discern the gravity of her health challenge. She applies a crystalline certainty to the necessity of living every day to the fullest because she has "better things to do than curl up on the sofa" and feel sorry for herself.

A wash of relief colored her account of the oncologist's determination that her particular lung cancer is the result of a rare genetic mutation. Hearing that, a person might sigh and think, Thank God it wasn't all those nights of karaoke, or the years of primal scream therapy, or one too many beers during college.

Peg says that with this trial, God must have a plan for her, something she is yet to discover. Maybe that plan includes volunteer work for the Make-a-Wish Foundation, a local project granting special wishes for children with deadly illnesses. She has long thought she might volunteer there after completing her tenure with the county, where she has twenty-eight years and nine months of service. She always expected to reach thirty, which earns the long-timer a coveted dinosaur pin, but now she qualifies for a medical retirement. Technically, she's not unable to work but her oncologist agrees that she is terminally ill, and that's enough for a Get Out of Jail card. What she really wants is that dinosaur pin.

For Peg there will be no cure, but perhaps containment, a concept that brings to mind the 2012 debate over how the U.S. should address Iran's efforts at developing nuclear weapons. Proponents of forestalling Iran's forward march argue that once the regime has weapons to kill people *en masse*, containment becomes the default goal. So now I'm wondering ... When humans contain within themselves the faculty for individual self-destruction (I'm thinking here of Peg's random cancer) why would we need weapons of mass destruction?

Human bodies contain billions of cells in constant flux, dividing and dying, dividing and dying. It seems that when left alone, a body is as likely to self-destruct as not. Why would we need faster, surer killing machines? Is it because we are all dying a million invisible internal deaths that we seek to control the external delivery of death as well?

Today, when the means for mass destruction appears on the horizon, outside forces are applied to prevent proliferation. That's containment. If the weapons rest quietly, awaiting the signal to maim and kill, people carry on, working and playing and making love and singing in the shower, never truly knowing when the next unseen, unbidden force will be unleashed. After it happens, *if* it happens, and we survive, we rise to our feet, knowing that there still exists a death force lurking just beyond sight. We work another shift, field phone calls from friends, and contemplate whether to take a medical retirement. We grant ourselves permission to live in the meantime.

↔

In our local paper there is now a column written by a senior citizen, Anne Pershing. Her column sports the slogan "Grandma with Attitude." It contains no groaning about the aging process, just observations from her senior perspective. I saved one with the title "Parenting a Hard Habit to Break." In it she notes that her kids are grown, sending her into parental withdrawal, and she needs to dial back the parenting mode she's been in for so long.

She distills advice from experts, or else paraphrases advice gleaned from elsewhere when she writes: "Love your grandchildren, but honor boundaries and refrain from attempting to constantly parent them. Don't be judgmental. Keep your own active social life, maintain your health, explore new interests." Best of all I like the line she ends with: "Treat your children with the same consideration you give your friends."

Anne, I don't even know you, but I like your style.

That column reminded me of an earlier conversation with PA, who always asks how we're faring as Tenders while sharing how tending works in her universe. We were at the Aroma Club, drinking our way to the bottom of a pot of tea, when she said, "I didn't sign up for this." It turned out she meant her father's attitude of entitlement. He seemed to expect that all things run only his way.

We agreed that he exercised a certain male prerogative typical of his generation. My maternal grandfather acted the same way. He liked, and expected, to be the rooster in charge of the house and its hens. I imagine that attitude wore my mother down. She was of a more modern generation, and besides, he had not been all that dedicated a father.

PA commiserated with me regarding my mother's assertion that a long tenure as parent and grandparent (no matter how distant from actual hands-on duties) grants a license to boss the younger generations. In that way she's like her dad.

There's a strategy that PA uses with her students who have learning and behavior challenges. It's called restating, or cognitive redirection. In it, the recipient reframes the other person's negative statement as a question. An example from my world would be, "Do you mean you don't believe I'm capable of washing the dishes, or is it that you don't want me to wash them?"

I am going to practice this reframing and see how it works.

↔

Dear AK,

So fleeting, those years we had, but they were grand, and when things faltered I had no ready answers. Where was my magic wand?

You were like the other, hidden half of me, better than a sister. I regret that we became lost to each other, twice. I know that I should be glad for the time we had. In this case, though, I could wish for a few more todays of laughing and talking and imagining the future as a banquet laid out before us. To you: luck, love, and smooth sailing.

↔

 To her credit, Momma has largely stopped complaining about our dinner menus, and I have quit anticipating that she will. She's become more agreeable about eating fish, especially if it's slathered with tartar sauce. She likes most kinds of salad, but almost no type of pasta. In the early days she would eat spaghetti, but no longer (even when the noodles are short and curly). Since anything beef suits her she might like me to prepare Beef Wellington, but I've drawn the line far south of that mark.

 Sometimes I overcook the fresh vegetables just for her, which increases her satisfaction while decreasing mine, but we've mostly reached a détente whereby we feed her good, nutritious food and I ignore any criticisms or insults.

 Tonight I offered spaghetti versus soup-and-sandwich. She chose the latter and I chose the former. As we were eating she reached for something, perhaps her knife. Over went her juice glass full of milk. What surprised me was not the quick tidal wave of white, but her response: "Oh, shit." Still that same small voice of hers, but an actual swear word. I smiled secretly in delight.

 Momma said: I try so hard not to have that happen.

 Me: Oh well, it'll clean up fine.

 Which, of course, it did.

↔

 Under his breath, Jim said: Four minutes.

 That's how much time had elapsed since I had offered to help his mother to the bathroom and she had declined. Sure enough, four minutes after she first declined my pre-dinner offer, she was ready.

 Should such reversals of decisions merit a wager, we would both bet the same side—in favor of sooner rather than later. Neither of us would get rich. Besides, it's like we wager already, the payoff being a wink and a grin.

↔

 I dislike cooking. Did I say that already? It's not that I'm entirely without talent; I've known people who couldn't properly boil water.

You could call me a decent cook, occasionally inventive, but I'd rather be reading or writing or weeding the garden, almost anything but standing at the stove.

Part of it, I'm sure, is that no matter my efforts, Momma rarely compliments anything that shows up on her plate. Gourmet, plain, fresh, frozen, it all seems to meet with the same response.

"What's this?" she'll say. Whoever has delivered her plate of food calls out each item. Her response is usually, "Huh."

Recently one of Momma's lady friends gave us some magazines she was done perusing, including two or three copies of *Bon Appétit*.

After her friend had gone, Momma paged through the gourmet magazine then said: Some of these dishes look really good.

Me: They do? Why don't you mark some of those pages and we'll make a grocery list. You can be the cook and I'll be your assistant, how's that?

Ellen who was sitting at the table with Momma, simply smiled and kept silent. She likes to cook less than I do.

No answer from Momma. I'm pretty sure she was thinking that sometimes I am such a grouch.

↔

February 23 ~

Momma had her undies on inside-out tonight when I helped her get ready for bed. No biggie. She can't tell the difference and her pantiliner will stick to either side of the cotton knit. It's my husband's fault, though, because for perhaps the first or second time ever our scheduled aide called in sick.

We knew since yesterday that Pat would stay home with her cold virus. My husband drew the short straw for morning duty. He's not game for it, but conceded that it was his turn.

Prior to preparations for Momma's bedside bath, Jim said: It doesn't seem right.

Me: Get over it. If you can clean her up after a bathroom emergency, you can hand her a soapy cloth and then a rinse cloth. She'll wash her own parts.

Jim: I guess so.

And he did. But I'm not about to tell him that her undies were on wrong. That would become an excuse to once again note, "I'm hoping that if I fuck things up enough I'll get fired from the job."

He's joking when he says that, except he's not. He'd love to get fired from this particular job ... but he'll never be that lucky.

Tonight I gathered up the trash from the kitchen and bathrooms and picked up the recyclables for the bin.

Jim jumped up from his spot in front of the golf tourney playing on TV. He said: I'll get that. I was going to get that.

Me, feigning indignity: Wouldn't want to interrupt your golf.

Him: I was going to do it, *really*.

He reached for my armload of stuff but I backed away.

Me: Don't make me drop this jar. It'll shatter.

Him: But, I was!

Me: Yeah, right. I'm getting credit for this.

That's another of our running jokes, announcing aloud the credit we expect for having accomplished a chore relating to our life with Momma. In all the years before this I don't think we ever joked about keeping track of who did what chores, but now we do. At least I think we're joking.

↔

More of February ~

Momma: Some days the phone rings off the hook and other days it doesn't ring at all.

Me: Just that one call from the furniture place.

Momma: What place?

Me: Well, I called them first. On my way through Sierra Valley yesterday I saw their sign. It said Furniture Sale.

Momma: You have furniture for sale?

Me: No.

Momma: Oh.

I explained to her how Jim's dresser and nightstand are about forty years old and I've never liked them. We've been thinking about purchasing newer, nicer stuff.

That's when I realized forty years is but a blink on Momma's timeline. She bought furniture once then kept it a lifetime. A child of the Great Depression, she saved every rubber band and greasy paper lunch sack.

A few weeks back she revealed a scrape on her leg that needed first aid attention. Momma said, as she often does: *I used to have* (in this case) some ointment to put on it. I don't know if that came over from the house.

Me: I did bring a lot of items from your bathroom.

I dug around and found the tube of Neosporin she was referencing. Something about its burgundy and saffron yellow color combination looked, well, not quite right. The package seemed familiar, but the expiration date on the crimped end of the tube read 04/94, which means, in theory, that it expired about eighteen years ago. For all I know, such products have a hundred year half-life, but being a wasteful sort I set it aside and retrieved a newer tube from my own bathroom.

She didn't know the difference, of course, would not have recognized one from the other. I dressed her wound and wrapped it with gauze. Then I tucked her old ointment away in a safe place. I'm going to keep it as a symbol of our current era: TM, also known as Tending Momma.

There you have it—the expanded version of our conversation about plans to replace forty-year-old furniture.

↔

On my way through a nearby California highway town I bought $20 worth of tickets for the three of us to play the Mega-what's-its-name lottery that links California to all those other states. The payoff had ballooned to $654 million by the time the numbers were pulled (three winners, none of them a Riley). A one-third share of that much dough would be about the right amount to keep a person in their old age, what with assisted living and nursing homes costing what they do.

I have long believed that a person's assets are meant to carry them to The End, not for squirreling away as a means to avoid paying one's own bills when the adult diapers get delivered or the paid Tender comes to help with bath time.

I sometimes hear people speak aloud about giving their money to their children and grandchildren before they get to the end so that their wealth stays in the family, which means, I suppose, that they will live on the dole during their feeblest years.

What a shitty plan. At another juncture some of those same folks would decry truly poor people as "welfare mothers" while expecting the next generation of taxpayers to foot the bill for their bibs and fanny wipes. All those assets sliding under the table or up the sleeves of complicit family members.

Momma's lifelong frugality fed her savings. Her money no longer goes for dinner dances or travel to foreign lands. No auto servicing or shopping for a flat screen TV. Her primary expense now is for home health aides.

I have suggested to my own mother that she'll need her savings and perhaps the proceeds from the sale of her house to finance her old age some day. She always says, "There's no old age guaranteed," and I always respond, "There's no reason you can't live a long time, even if your health is failing and you're unhappy about it."

I don't yet fear that she will donate her remaining assets to the Red Cross for Haitian relief, though she might someday. Should that happen, I doubt the Red Cross will send any of it back to pay for her medical bills or living expenses.

↔

March 14 ~
Over a cup of tea, my friend PA told me more about her Pop.

Her mother died almost two years ago; in the years since, her father found a new love, someone who has been both companion and watcher over his health. He's eighty-something, she's a younger eighty-something or perhaps late seventies, so she was the one who drove their recently acquired motor home for a journey to Florida, two more snowbirds among the flock already there. As it turned out, they had two or three months of relaxation, then something went terribly wrong with his health. His legs gave out first and then came a stroke.

PA and her siblings made a plan, the short explanation of it being that within two or three weeks they flew their Pop home via air ambulance at a cost of $17,000.

"It was worth it," she said. She knew (as did her siblings) that her father wanted to be home again. Her brother flew to Florida and drove the lady friend home in the mo-ho. The family's four children responded according to their abilities and if more assistance is needed, they will call upon other relatives who live near to Pop's hometown.

PA, who teaches at a 12-month school, had regularly been spending her off-track time flying halfway across the U.S. to help with various projects at the family's lakeside RV park. When we met over tea she reported that her father was now holding his own, though not improving. She said that if his life is nearing its end, she will harbor no regrets for things left unsaid because she never withheld her feeling. She has for years made clear her love for him. That knowledge gives her peace.

She *did* look at ease. Like someone who knows she could not have reversed her father's desire for companionship or travel, nor would she have tried.

I'm not sure there's a nicer view to a treasured friend than to see her at peace with the next stage of her life—assuming the mantle of family elder as her remaining parent takes his leave.

↔

KH and I are agreed. We want to grow up to be Maxine, that irrepressible, sarcastic senior citizen of Hallmark greeting card fame. We will wear our robes and bunny slippers all day and crack jokes at the expense of young whippersnappers (*there's* a word for you) because we'll subscribe to a quote credited to Marilyn Monroe: "The longer you last, the less you care."

Of course MM lasted fairly well by Hollywood standards, but Reno is a smidge easier on people. If Marilyn had stuck around these parts after making her last film (*The Misfits*), she might have married a rancher and had a life with fewer spotlights burning holes in her candy shell. Some of those ranchers have pretty big spreads, but that kind of life only qualifies as glamorous if you go in for Wranglers and Tony Lamas, hand-tooled saddles and line dancing after the ranch rodeo.

It's too late for MM, but if KH and I start practicing soon, we'll be good at our Maxine-ness by the time we're old enough to get away with it.

↔

Psycho Dog bit me today. Bet you can guess how I felt about that.

↔

Week of March 18 ~

In the mail this week came an offer addressed to Momma from Progressive Insurance. Because she is such a safe motorcycle driver they would like to insure her motorcycle. (First a dealer tried to sell her a bike; now she needs insurance for the rocket bike she didn't buy.)

We had a laugh before Jim tossed it in the recycle bin. I was tempted to snap a picture of her in her wheelchair, white curls shining in the sun, and send it to them with a message saying, "Thanks for the offer. Maybe next year."

↔

In a telephone conversation today, my mother said that one of my brothers had used the term "old lady" in conversation. She took offense and has e-mailed him with instructions not to call her for a while. Electronic messages will be fine, but no phone calls until she cools off.

According to her, he could have used the term elderly, or else senior citizen, as she knows that's what she is. But not *old*. She doesn't think of herself as old.

I could have pointed out that she sometimes says, "It's hell to get old," but I didn't. I was kind of glad not to be the one in trouble with her. This time.

Maybe I'm wrong about the "old" I've been using. I had assigned it a position at the opposite end of young, by which I did not mean to infer any infirmities or inherent value, simply age.

My Webster's provides definitions that include "persisting from another time," and "advanced in years of age." It clarifies that old may refer to actual or relative length of existence.

Next I looked up "elderly." My dictionary gives "rather old," and "old-fashioned."

I think I'll keep those definitions to myself.

↔

Dear Sweet P,

Wasn't it grand how we found ourselves in the same place at the same time and then fabricated more opportunities to spend time together? All those volunteer projects and special events. The summer yard sales where we junked for treasures, the discussions about grandchildren over deli sandwiches, the sewing lessons! (You're a natural.)

You positively glow when you mention adored, adorable D, echoing your affection for your grown children, but with an extra dash of awe.

Do you know how much I admire your teaching work plus your dedication and resolve in the face of daily challenges presented by bureaucratic folderol, stressed-out colleagues, and wacky parents? You seem to possess incredible reserves of calm and an uncanny ability to soothe and comfort.

Yours is a poet's soul without the black clouds. Something about knowing you fills me up. Allotted just one word, I would label you "kind," hoping it could pull duty for the others belonging in the Sweet P string—generous, unassuming, talented, content, faithful—words that can hold their heads high when paired with your name. You express such delight at the success of friends and strangers. You are a blessing in my life.

↔

March 24 ~

Today I was tending to Momma in the bathroom. We agreed that it was an unfortunate day for toileting business.

Momma drew a deep breath and said: It's like a baby.

I paused. Her non-sequiturs can refer to a newspaper story from hours ago or a movie she watched the previous night. Sometimes a reference might hark back to a phone conversation she's had with her sister.

Me: Umm ...

Then I realized what she meant.

Momma: Kind of.

Honesty seemed called for, so I said: Yeah, kind of.

Here's the rub. If she were a younger person with some terminal illness other than Life, and within that illness she experienced toileting troubles, or became choosy about foods, or was cranky from her constant pain, we would deal with it. Par for the course.

But elders do not think of themselves as ill, even though what they suffer from is terminal. Because we euphemize the reality, the symptoms of aging can strike us as unfortunate or just plain disagreeable (I admit to sometimes feeling discouraged as I tend to the symptoms).

I delivered Momma to her sofa where she became engrossed in reruns of Storage Wars Texas while feeding peanuts to Psycho Dog. I rinsed her panties, compression stockings, and trousers before hanging them all to dry above her bathtub. When dry they'll go into the laundry, of which I am the mistress.

↔

Late March ~

Call me "fussbudget." That's the term Jim says his mother assigned me last night when I was out bowling and my brother called. Momma always wants to know who is calling, and also sometimes the talking points. Jim has been known to say, "None of your business, Miss Snoopypants."

In this case my brother was reporting our mother's awful headaches of late. He was wondering if she might have an aneurism.

Momma asked Jim if my mother had told me about her headaches. Jim thought not. Momma said that would probably be because I'm such a fussbudget. When later he reported her comment to me, we laughed about it.

At 1:30 a.m. I was awakened by a voice in Momma's bedroom. She seemed to be talking to someone. I lay listening for a while until eventually she rang her bell and I went to see what was up. Pickle Dog had thrown up a bunch of frothy white fluid with little chunks in it and was standing at the foot of the bed. She wouldn't budge.

Momma looked up at me from her reclining position and said: I think she doesn't feel well.

Me: I guess not. She's thrown up on your blanket, as far from her sleeping place as she can get.

Momma: I was wondering why she was so restless.

Me: She probably feels better now. It looks like potato chips. Did you feed her potato chips again today?

Momma: Yes. I suppose so.

Me: I saw she didn't eat her dinner, so that might be why. It's time to stop feeding her potato chips, okay?

Momma, sounding weary: Okay.

I cleaned up the mess and Pickle Dog climbed back under the covers with her boss. Once again I'm the one who takes the fun out of things. After all, Pickle Dog is Momma's little friend and lover, entitled to potato chips no matter the consequences.

I went back to bed. My husband spoke up from his side: What was that about?

I told him.

Husband: Sorry about that. You can wake me, you know.

Me: If I have to wake you then I'm awake enough to get up and have a look. But maybe I *will*, next time.

It was the next day that I learned that I'm a fussbudget (a fine, old-fashioned word). I've decided that sometimes that's what this tending job calls for.

↔

First of April ~

I have two scribbled notes in blue ink that read, "Wresting the car away" and "Prying Mother out of hers."

Oddly enough, I'm typing this within days of a conversation with Momma that almost, sort of, pointed to that subject. Here's how it went on a day this last week:

Momma asked whether I had more bowling to come. Once again I explained how last night was what's called the "position round," in which teams compete for 1st place, 2nd place, 3rd and so on. I've been bowling for the first time in a mixed league, which simply means coed. We built our team in what I think of as true mixed fashion: two women and two men. In this case, the two women are middle-aged mothers and the men on our team are my friend's twenty-something son and the son's best friend, both nice guys, both athletic. This is the first year for the two young guys while she and I have bowled together for six or seven years.

We did discover that the mixed leagues are brimming with scratch bowlers, typically men. Some of them bowl so well they don't even have handicaps, which in bowling, as with golf, are formulated to level the playing field. A bowling handicap is useful when competing against scratch bowlers in the same way that a golf handicap levels the field against Tiger Woods. No matter. We have decided to have fun regardless of the outcome.

Back to Momma. Her naptime was over and I brought a bowl of water to her bedside for the washing of her hands. I explained in answer to her question that I have one more Friday night of bowling, which will be for fun only, not for prizes. And we'll have a potluck.

Momma paused then said: These are your golden years.

I helped her into her gray sweater jacket before she plopped down into her wheelchair.

Me: You mean the bowling and all.

Momma: Uh-huh.

Me, taking a comb to her curls: I guess that means you're past your golden years.

Momma: Yes.

Then she added: I don't recommend it.

Me: I guess you'll just have to carry on anyway.

Later I thought that I wouldn't have taken my recent past or my current home life for golden years, even though I am lucky enough to have a flexible work schedule and comfortable digs. I putter in the garden on sunny days. My car runs fine and in it I drive like a person in love with the road.

Thus far, my years with the sunniest glow were probably those following our daughter's college graduation and the first few years after we retired. Then about seven years ago, Momma began needing almost daily assistance from us in her own home and that changed the catch-lights of our days.

I suppose our golden years may resume again at some future point. If they do not, I will have underestimated how much chauffeuring, hair dressing, fanny wiping, laundressing, chief cook and bottle washing, medicine rationing, wound dressing, pedicuring, dog supervising, disinfecting, and vomit eradication in the wee hours they might include.

In her 50s and 60s, Momma had a share of extra fine years when she travelled to various parts of the world with lady friends. That was before I knew Jim. She had long since been widowed, which must have clouded plenty of her days (or years). In her 70s and beyond, she stuck closer to home.

I mentioned this to Jim that night, the conversation about golden years, and he said she had used the same term with him, mentioning also that the golden years are when you still have your driver's license. And those commercials, he said, the ones with sunsets, sailboats, and two seniors holding hands ...

Red sky at morning, sailors take warning

... they never mention all the health problems that come with the territory.

Then he said he hopes I get a break between tending his mother and tending mine.

My hopes exactly.

↔

April 19 ~

A substitute aide came today. As she worked she described an elderly man she tends on a regular basis. He gets 24/7 care, but he also has family members living close by who see him daily. The son comes and parcels out the meds. The daughter-in-law stays over three times a week with the man, a 97-year-old. Sally said that the elder had experienced a stroke, that's partly how he came to be a client. She noted that some of the other workers do not want to work with this old guy. "He's cranky," she said. "But I don't mind. I don't let it bother me. I figure, he's ninety-seven! He's earned it."

I was thinking right about then that she had Momma sitting adjacent to her and Momma is that old. I'd rather the person I'm tending didn't think she had earned the right to a bad attitude. It seems one thing to be cranky from pain or because your body parts have just plain worn out. That's what I imagine 97 might be like: the teeth in your mouth ground flat, the teeth of your body's gears sheared of their pointy parts. Such challenges might induce the blues or a certain amount of frustration, but to have *earned* being cranky? That's dangerous territory.

Proposing a "right" to crankiness suggests that living a long time bestows meanness privileges. In that case, everyone who makes it halfway or more (me, for instance) gets to be cranky, or obstinate, or mean, roughly half of the time. Or else they get to act half-cranky all of the time. I can picture a world of people exercising the privilege of being unpleasant to others.

I am a fair hand at accommodating another person's pain and misery. I understand that life's upsides are balanced by downsides. First-hand experience will teach you that. But *earnings* are relative to what we have *accomplished*. If we earn the right to be cranky through sheer longevity, by living long enough, something is out of kilter.

Other aides have told Sally that her client can't speak, but she says he communicates with her. As she demonstrated his grunts and nods, and single, audible words I was reminded of my grandfather, who lost his ability to speak clearly after a stroke. He could talk, but not using any pattern of words the rest of us could recognize as sentences, just a single word here or there. He got by because he could understand what others said, and he could still count money and all. If he wrote a note, though, the words came out as nonsense, the sort of "faux Greek" that graphic artists set into a rough advertising layout where the real advertising text will eventually go, nonsensical combinations of consonants and vowels grouped together like so many strangers lined up at the curb to signal taxis.

My mother tended her parents for years. When I visited during that time, I detected that my grandmother had retreated into herself as my grandfather tried to control my mother, who was there doing the dirty work. He wanted Mother there to help them, to do what they could not, but he wanted the work done *his* way. He was the boss, couldn't she see that hadn't changed? They butted heads, which may have satisfied him but was not healthy for her.

At one point, fed up, she packed her bags and drove three days to reach Reno, spending two nights in truck stops with a handgun under her seat. Later, though, she went back.

My grandfather probably thought that by living into his 80s he'd earned the right to rule his own house, regardless of the fact that his daughter was tending to his needs the way he had never tended to hers. He could be charming when it suited him, though I doubt he squandered much charm on Mother. If she thought he ought to act more cooperative and grateful, and less bossy and entitled, she would have been right.

↔

Dear KH,

You said once that you chose me for your friend, but really, I chose you too. For your wacky sense of humor (no portrait will ever compare with your pinhead photo), your obsession for documenting things in triplicate, and how you provide succor to crazy, frenetic, and/or disabled friends.

I've been try to account for what binds us as friends. Not simply your impressive collections of diet books and maps of Nevada. Not only your acute sense of history. Could it be our shared affinity for chocolate chip cookies, igneous rocks, and dogs with personality? Perhaps it's our mutual disregard for rules and conventions while strictly obeying almost all of them. How about our shared belief in the power of disbelief? Then there's your love of the high desert and appreciation of watery places and my love of the coast and appreciation of the desert. I'm sure it's all of the above.

I know I told you this once but it still holds true, that for as much as I admired Shirley as a thoughtful, creative woman, I knew she was special because you cared about her and believed in her, and deeply grieved her illness and death. Because she mattered to you, she mattered a little extra to me. Your heart is bigger than you let on.

I can honestly say that there is nobody more fun than you with whom to tramp through a flooded horse pasture or debate the merits of Conboie's undertakings.

I've been working toward a badge for spontaneity (you surely earned yours long ago). When we become our grandmothers, hopefully while occupying your old-folks commune, we'll don our many badges and parade around as if they make us seem somehow more ... accomplished. No matter that we will have forgotten what they stand for.

↔

I've given up on following the vet's instructions for Pickle Dog: to use both the canned dog food and kibble for senior dogs, products formulated with less protein. Pickle Dog won't eat them and it's no longer worth my mental health to fix meals that she refuses to eat, after which she slinks around acting deprived. Then Momma asks if we can give her something else to eat. We throw out the first meal, wash the bowl, and start all over. The dog grows skinnier and more persnickety while I grow less hospitable toward her (and lose no weight). So be it. People food plus high protein dog food for her, as it is and always shall be, amen. The little rat will be smiling when her kidneys give out and I'll save my tears for a more agreeable pet.

↔

The TV-watching, Coke-and-potato-chip hour arrives just after naptime, typically the time for watching Judge Judy, but it's the weekend so at 3:40 I find Momma watching an infomercial touting workout tapes that teach boot camp tactics for burning fat and sculpting abdominal muscles. Lots of sweaty, buff men and women, especially the men. There were a few testimonials, but mostly it was fabulous-looking young people doing squat-jumps and push-ups, and all those gleaming bodies!

They don't make 'em like they used to

Me: This is an infomercial. Do you want me to find you something else to watch?
Momma: No. It's kind of interesting.
I was amused. She usually likes Little House on the Prairie and classic movies where things move slowly and no-one curses and they occasionally show an ankle or perhaps a forearm below a rolled shirtsleeve. Clearly *today* she prefers taut glutes and washboard abs, short-shorts on the girls and shirtless men, like a romance on steroids but without a plot.

After that paid programming concluded she watched an infomercial for Ronco knives. That one, she said, was interesting too. Tomatoes sliced thin as paper! Herbs chopped fine as chef's hair! I'm going to quit assuming I know what she likes.

↔

May begins ~

I've always thought of myself as healthy. I look healthy, with body parts that move relatively well and all my fingers and toes. I have all my teeth and my hair hasn't yet turned gray, though I sometimes wonder why not.

I feel younger than my years but there's an occasional sensation of my engine cooling after a long hot ride, with a click-tick-tick as various components begin contracting in the cooling dusk.

When I was young I felt invincible. Didn't we all? In those days nobody talked about what it was like to grow old, at least they didn't talk about it to us young people, or speak about it within our hearing. The aging, disease, and dementia processes were all hush-hush. Of course we didn't talk about sex or religion either.

If you looked at the list of all my ailments and complaints, it would be chock full of piddly shit, none worth crying over. I did, however, spend last night in the ER with chest pain. I had been sitting with a writer-colleague who was working at his laptop, me twisting hard right to show him a few formatting and layout techniques for his book. When I stood, the pain kicked in.

The ER folks drew blood and ran tests and gave me drugs to dissolve under my tongue. My injury turned out to be an irritation of the connective tissue in the chest wall. I've never sneezed and thrown out my back, but now I've twisted wrong and traumatized my sternum. Go figure.

It's clearer to me than ever that I'm at that witching age when I am headed, however gradually, toward pumpkinhood. That is not to confuse the nature of my damaged goods with Peg's stage-IV cancer, or my great-nephew's double pulmonary artery surgery—at the tender age of three.

All I mean is that we're all cut from the same magnificently flawed cloth.

May 6 ~

Jim: I hate that dog. I know you know that but I just had to say it. I'm probably overreacting, but I hate her.

I knew which dog he meant and by now, you do too.

↔

I have begun fantasizing about calling it quits. I could, you know. I could just say to Jim, "I can't do this anymore." He would pause and formulate a reply and then he'd say … What would he say? He might say, "All right, we've done our best. I understand if you're done." Or he might make a case for holding out a little longer. He might offer to take on more of the duties (which he ought to be doing anyway since it's *his* mom we're tending). There might be some negotiating. He would know, though, that I'm not one for drama and hyperbole. No hysterics, no overwrought exclamations of how I can't handle a particular task or challenge when in fact I can. If I ever made such a declaration, he would divine its nature.

One of our aides has a step-mother with Parkinson's, which makes her creaky, somewhat forgetful, and often in need of assistance for ordinary tasks. Pat regularly goes over to help, which is in addition to her night shifts in one of the assisted living facilities in town, which is in addition to having at home an adult special needs daughter.

Pat's family has hinted that she give up her other work to tend her step-mom. To me, Pat said, "No way. I don't believe people should take care of their own relatives." If anyone would know, she ought to.

Back to Jim. If I ever hit him with those five little words, he'll know I've given it a lot of thought before coming to the conclusion that I've reached the end.

↔

Mother's Day ~

Floor dusting, toilet scrubbing, food prep, table polishing, etc. because our daughter is in town from law school. She, her boyfriend, and her uncle came for dinner and conversation. It was Momma we were feting. Who was it who said Mother's Day is a day of rest for mothers? Or maybe that doesn't apply to stepmothers. The good news is that I'm not in this alone. Yesterday Jim washed the kitchen floors and entryways, and mowed the lawns.

Together he and I set the table and prepared dinner and served it, and cleaned up afterwards. And we tended to Momma, who had announced yesterday that tonight she would have ice cream with her cake (a woman after my own heart, anticipating dessert for the next day's dinner).

Me, yesterday: No, Ma'am. You and I will skip the ice cream.

Momma: How come?

I drew close and spoke in a low voice: Because it will give you loose bowels and I don't want to clean up a bathroom emergency if I can help it.

You are, perhaps, thinking me harsh, but Momma is very direct in the way she instructs people to bring her this, or put that over there. For some reason she is particularly dense when it comes to changes in her tolerance for foods she used to indulge with impunity. She also used to manage a surgeon's office, spend a night on the town, drive everywhere—even to Eugene, Oregon—mow her own lawn, weed her gardens, and preside over the activities of an Eastern Star chapter. But she hasn't done those things in many moons. Not only do some things change as the years pile up, but all things change to one degree or another.

I think she has a better memory for her lactose intolerance than she lets on. She'd like for things to be not this way. Believe me, I would too, but things are not what they used to be.

↔

When I was young, I always felt older than my years. Not *old* as in ready for The Home, just older than my allotted years, so that when I was in my young teens I felt I had outgrown the childish things I had once practiced and that others my age were still practicing. At eighteen I could pass for twenty-one. Those were the disco days, when music clubs were happy to welcome young women into their darkened, pulsing interiors.

In a strange twist of luck I became twenty-one when I was only eighteen. Eighteen was the age at which California's Department of Motor Vehicles issued a license with the driver's portrait taken facing the camera instead of in profile. Having turned eighteen I went in to renew my license.

To my astonishment the license they gave me showed my age as twenty-one. That was the Pleistocene era, before computers, when documents were typed manually. In this case some overworked, underappreciated public servant had made a simple mistake.

I don't recall immediately recognizing my big score, but soon enough I noticed and naturally rejoiced. The subsequent three years were smooth sailing through the local nightclub scene.

What, you might ask, happened three years later when my fabulous license was due for renewal? I simply went to the DMV and explained how they had goofed. The counter clerk snatched the license from my hand and called for a supervisor. They bent together, trying to discern how I could have so perfectly counterfeited a laminated document. Without cause for arrest, they issued me a corrected license. That's how it was that at eighteen I became twenty-one and then three years later became twenty-one again.

I still dig paisley, some tie-dye, and poofy page-boy haircuts (for women only, please)

My lucky driver's license notwithstanding, at twenty-ish, I felt older than my years, as if I had already reached my mid-twenties. And so it went. I first married a man three years older. My next significant other was six years older. My second marriage was to a man nine years my senior. I continue to straddle the decades.

↔

Speaking of ancient times, I miss the 1960s. Or rather, I *missed* them the first time around, which makes me nostalgic for what I was too young for then—what I think of as the halcyon hippie days, the leading edge of the women's movement, and the kaleidoscopic shifts in culture, fashion, and home design. Though I did get to see a black light or two, I was half a pint too young and without the funds necessary to seriously party, become an activist, or sit in and tune out.

Though I am long past miniskirts, I still love the look of them. I liked the swinging 60s' hairdos, the bold patterns (paisley!), bellbottoms, and muscle cars.

Although the happening called Woodstock happened without me, I learned to love the music it spawned. My tastes in music sprang from what older kids were into, my brothers included. Though I didn't own albums, I had a transistor radio and a record player for my small collection of vinyl 45s, and knew the words to all the popular songs.

Maybe what I wanted was to be a part of what was happening around me. Instead I felt like I was being left behind, stuck with the constraints of the under-aged. Back then I thought I knew plenty. Later I realized how much I needed to learn. Now I am certain that I am losing some of what I once knew, *plus*, I'll never know as much as I could wish to.

↔

Dear LM,

Comment vas-tu? That's roughly the extent of my French, but such conversations we've had in English! So many questions and musings, so few universal answers, just those that suited us personally, which is what we must have meant to gain. All that thinking out loud, the scrim of our divergent backstories lifted for an hour as we parsed the contradictions inherent in U.S. politics, faith, economics, and human relations.

You have been my source for all things French and Italian, mutual lover of NPR and the BBC. I wonder if one day we will travel to Paris so that you can guide me through your beloved arrondissements dotted by cathedrals, cafés and bookstores, The Conciergerie, the crowds of Montmartre, Tuileries Gardens, and along the Seine, where we would smile at young lovers as they stroll.

Of course we will visit Shakespeare and Company and take time to walk a few narrow streets lined with weathered buildings graced by iron railings. We should also journey to the top of the Eiffel Tower to watch car lights reflecting on the rain-slick streets below.

While we shared pots of tea just a few miles from home, I pictured you in a Paris café, porcelain demitasse of espresso in hand, conversing with the waiter and perhaps the gentleman at the next table. You ordered a crocque monsieur for old time's sake.

Had I won the lotto we would have already toured those places, you in your element and me wide-eyed within the penumbra of your joy at being there once again. There we might find the comfort of much-loved old places under our feet and in our eyes.

Perhaps we will journey there as seniors, wearing sweaters and sensible slacks, but chic in black, a touch of Hepburn in our smiles.

↔

May continues ~

I ran into a friend and her sister today at a downtown bakery called Kyle's Sweet Treats. (Did I mention I've given up baking in favor of buying baked goods?) As it often does, small talk turned to family matters. I mentioned tending a 97-going-on-98-year-old and of course their eyes bugged out. Happens all the time.

The sister said that she often wonders what will become of her in future years, when she's old. She wrinkled her nose as if unable to imagine her two grown sons caring for their elderly mother.

Me: My husband is a son, and he is. We are.

Her: Yes, but he's got a wife who's willing to do the work too.

Her implication was that she doesn't expect to be so lucky. She might be right. Jim told me once that he would not have brought his mother into his home without a willing partner. At the time I took him to mean he wouldn't have had he been a bachelor, but of course, a married person wouldn't bring their parent home to live as casually as they might a new puppy.

In the sweet shop I explained how I hope to afford a helper someday so that I can be an old lady in my own home, but I forgot to suggest that they might join me in KH's commune, where a bunch of us childless old people will look out for each other.

↔

PA's father died this month while she was in Michigan visiting. His children (her siblings) and grandkids were present. They had made him comfortable in the living room of the lodge of the family's lakefront RV park. While conversations ebbed and flowed around him, he could look out at the water he had spent so many years living alongside. There was also music, and laughter.

She told me again what she had mentioned before, that she had always expressed her love to him. Even when he couldn't any longer communicate or she wasn't certain he understood what people were saying, she knew that he knew she loved him.

Her stories about growing up warmed me. Stories about his zest for life (her mother was less effusive, more critical and demanding). How he would hook a mattress to the back of a vehicle and pull it around in the snow with the kids riding atop its springy surface. How he was always up for the children's schemes and adventures. "Well, Sis," he would say to PA, "let's try it. Why not?" She and her siblings were trusted by their parents to be responsible and to find happiness as adults.

As she puts it, her father has journeyed home now. She knows peace in that.

↔

My mother is what she calls "safety conscious." She carries two sets of house keys, car keys, and gate keys, one set in each pants pocket. Still, somehow she managed to lock herself out of her house while unloading groceries from her car, which was parked in her detached garage adjacent to the alley at the back of her property.

Her practice is to lock the house each time she goes out the door for any reason. This means that if she were really in trouble, perhaps worried about someone approaching from the alley while she moved the hose-end sprinkler to a new position, she'd have to unlock her house to reach safety. Or make a run for it to the street beyond, and she's no runner.

Anyway, she told me about it when I called and we shared a laugh. She had gone to a neighbor's house to use the phone to call a locksmith. The locksmith staff knew her, of course. *By name.*

Her ideal house would sport a fenced yard containing a large police dog, surrounded by a moat with a drawbridge and one or two crocodiles. Oh, and bars on the windows.

↔

Mid-May ~

Jim's new dresser and nightstand came today in a delivery from Sierra Valley Furniture, the young Amish delivery man being one of their artisans. The pieces are cherry wood with a stain called "Michael's," and they are so well built they will last through Jim's remaining days.

We rolled Momma into our bedroom to show her the goods. She thought it a fine set, though she was probably thinking how his old stuff had been serviceable.

I showed her how the drawers open and close on slides, silent and sure. She's never seen the likes of these. Her house was built in the late 1930s and she and Jim's father furnished it with pieces they acquired early in their marriage, meaning the 1940s and decades once removed. By the time she joined us here she could barely open any drawer in her house, such was her lack of strength to work those wood-on-wood drawers. Even she could work these.

↔

Memorial Day approaches and Momma has repeated a recent idea. That's how she says it: "I have an idea." She wondered if I would secure some artificial flowers to take to the cemetery for adorning the family crypts containing her aunt Ennie, uncle Fred, and mother Amsie. Might I have any plastic flowers stored in the basement, you know, some I had purchased in my travels, or else had retained from those last stored in her home?

I confessed to her that I had no plastic flowers. She wanted some "fresh plastic flowers" to be put in the mausoleum, and to keep it from becoming complicated, I could just set them on the floor in front of the crypts.

The mausoleum has no ladder, just a lightweight pole for removing and replacing the vases, but I gave up trying to explain the futility of leaving flowers on the floor in front of some stranger's crypt, and assured her that Jim and I would purchase bouquets and perform our duties.

Momma described how her mother-in-law, Zoe, fussed over, *insisted upon*, fresh flowers for the graves she tended in the Carson City cemetery, though she didn't have the money to spend that way.

We agreed that providing fresh flowers must have been a source of pleasure for Zoe; she found comfort in her approach to honoring the dead.

A confession: I have been known to soften the sharp elbows of complete honesty with a fib or a bit of indirection. We all do it. "You've cut your hair. Nice." Or, "New jacket? What a great color." I used to nod my head and tell Momma, "Sure, I'll take those coats," then deliver her items to Goodwill.

The question of cemetery duty could have been one of those times that turn on a bit of fiction. Any flowers last placed there remain perpetual bloomers, immortal in their plastic crypt vases. For some reason, people either rarely, or *never*, steal fake flowers from crypts, and really, would Momma ever discern which flowers, which colors, which bouquets were new versus those with some age on them? She hasn't been to the mausoleum in a decade and I'll wager she won't ever visit it again.

It is not our family's custom to regularly visit cemeteries or orchestrate memorial celebrations for the long-dead. We simply clean any weeds from the Riley family's Carson City gravesites and place a few artificial flowers on the headstones there. I think I've been the only one in the last few years to even check on the condition of the Carson City graves. Strictly speaking they're not even my people. I never met a one of them.

As to my own future death, I'm determined to avoid rotting away in a box stuck in the ground or in a wall. If more people knew the biological processes taking place after death, the way aerobic and anaerobic microbes reduce a corpse to a stinking soup, they might not think a traditional burial such a benign end. I refer you to the book *Stiff* by Mary Roach. It contains the type of information about what happens after death that we tidy Americans who are not morticians or coroners generally relegate to someone else's sphere of knowledge. To put it delicately, what comes after death is ... messy.

No burial for me. Make mine a cremation, please, and scatter the flakey bits of me to the desert, or garden, or sea. Perhaps a single molecule will feed the renewal of our planet's life forces and that will be my dusty legacy.

↔

Jim and I are fans of the San Francisco Giants, though I guess I'm the least fan of all, for as much as I like the roar of a ballpark and even a bit of baseball on TV, it doesn't mean enough for me to memorize any stats or retain the names of the rotating crop of players. I grew up with brothers who were fans of the Giants and the Oakland Athletics, a trait learned at the altar of our father's love of the game. Those were the days of Willie McCovey, Willie Mays, and Stan Musial. Since my husband is a Giants fan, during the boys-of-summer season there is often a baseball game playing in the background of our evening at home.

Buster Posey, the Giants' first-string catcher, is back in action after rehab following a 2011 injury during a smash-up at the plate. Tonight he was hitless. My husband provided some color commentary.

Jim: He had shingles not too long ago, is probably still trying to get over them.

Me: He's a young guy! With shingles? That's kind of strange.

Momma chimed in: That's what killed Cecelia.

She meant her dear old friend, dead two years ago at the age of 98. Cecilia had had shingles in her last few years, and was miserable with them, but so far as I know that's not what killed her.

Jim and I had a chuckle later over how history gets revised through the singular details that a person latches onto, in this case Momma's focus on how shingles can be devastatingly painful. I'm sure Momma herself feared a visit from the shingles-demon and so it became the ogre that killed her friend.

At ninety-seven you don't lose as many friends each year as you did in decades past, maybe one or two folks from around the old neighborhood, or people you once knew in business. That's because at such an age, you have outlived a majority of your cohorts. Those left belong to a younger generation who will wave goodbye as your elderboat sails into the inky night, all the more reason to cultivate friends of various ages. One needn't be purposeful about gathering people with a younger mindset, balancing one generation against others, just willing to hold open the door for a few opportunities.

Still, Momma has expressed her wish for an Eastern Star memorial service, and we will oblige on some future day ("Not to be mean," said my husband recently, "but I think she'll live to one hundred without even blinking. She's like the Energizer Bunny.")

Order of the Eastern Star is a ladies' organization associated with the Freemasons that sprouted back in the day when many civic groups embraced Christianity for their guiding principles. I have witnessed two or three of their public ceremonies, which contain prayers and obvious symbolic references to Christianity.

Jim's mom is not particularly religious. I once asked whether she had been attracted to Eastern Star's religiosity. She said she hadn't given it much thought. Clearly, though, the group itself has meant a great deal to her. During her many decades as a member, she ascended through the ranks to a position known as Worthy Grand Matron, which bestows upon the holder both prestige and great responsibility.

A few of the remaining Eastern Star members will remember her, and the rest will turn out in force for a memorial to a past Grand Matron.

↔

Early June ~

Took a late morning walk with my newly-repaired knee and came across Marlene, a neighborhood acquaintance who will turn 93 soon. Long ago I thought of 93 as quite old, but in retrospect, it now seems youngish-old.

Marlene was sitting in her brown BMW, having just checked on the welfare of someone else in the neighborhood. She left the car running and sat behind the wheel as we visited. Though she has had two knees and one hip replaced, she walks her standard poodle almost daily and claims that her bionic body parts "work great." She has many friends but no relatives left alive (two brothers are gone, both smokers). To the news of my arthroscopic knee surgery she said she would encourage everyone to get their damaged parts repaired or replaced—to not let pain keep them from moving about.

Marlene has an upright bearing and distinguished good looks. I have seen her wearing a pale Delft-blue wool car coat over black slacks. White-haired, she cuts quite a figure with her gray dog. I'm always in jeans or warm-ups when I walk the neighborhood, a ball cap pulled low to keep my hair from flying, or a wide-brimmed gardening hat to shield me from the sun.

Though Marlene appears stately from a distance, moving at a measured pace, up close you may notice food stains on her coat or blouse.

There's a bit of comfort in imagining that the aging process brings with it less care about the state of our laundry or whether the dog gets up on the bed; and a bit of concern that we'll not only willingly relinquish control but unintentionally lose control over many details of our lives. I am vain enough to hope that to my very last breath I will maintain my grip on the control of my own affairs, health, and pleasure pursuits, but realistic enough to predict that I won't.

Marlene manages somehow to keep things together, keep moving, and keep motoring. Her driver's license was renewed two years ago without a road test. She motioned to her left eye. "Not so good, this one. They must have decided that my right eye made up for it."

My paternal grandfather drove until reaching 85, his last year of life. He was a Search & Rescue volunteer and had driven heavy equipment in his younger days, cutting paths for the installation of power lines across forested ridges of California's Feather River Canyon. But he also took nitroglycerine for his heart, had taken nitro for thirty or forty years. The need for such a medication indicated a potentially fatal flaw in his ticker and I didn't like that potential.

While we sped downhill from his mountain town of Paradise to the city of Chico below, Gramps would chat amiably. His company was pleasant but I would be gritting my teeth against the possibility, the inevitability, of his heart slamming to a sudden stop.

At that speed I might have had a few seconds in which to grab the wheel and try to lift his foot from the accelerator. But I always suspected that we would flame out like Thelma and Louise, sailing off the highway, over the side ... sayonara.

It wasn't his heart that killed Gramps; he died of emphysema. Near the end he confessed that had he known he would live so long, he would have taken better care of himself.

↔

I have long been drawn to children and old people. Even odd people. I don't know why. Maybe it's because I raised no babies of my own, or because people of my grandparents' age seemed calm and affable. I never thought of my own family as odd, though we must have been; isn't everyone odd in some ordinary way?

Having no true eccentrics in my immediate universe I enjoy observing the behavior of people who are a bit off the main rail. I can also find them interesting to talk with. Perhaps I learn something from them—like how to let go a little, be less controlled or controllable, and how to imagine other worldviews.

One example is Harold, a gentleman who years ago lived three blocks west and north of us. He was still practicing law at 80-something, taking pro-bono cases for workers who were challenging or defending against their employers, wrongful termination cases and the like.

Not only did he live in the neighborhood, he seemed mostly *of* the neighborhood. By that I mean that I regularly observed him ambling along the streets in our part of town. It's an older neighborhood that lacks sidewalks for fairly long stretches, the yards or gardens reaching out to nuzzle the curbs and gutters. Pedestrians take to the margins of the driving lanes to get around.

That first day I spotted Harold as I turned uphill onto Palisade Drive; he was a bent figure in the distance. I was moving at a rapid pace, but rather than pass him I fell into step alongside.

Eyes on his shoes, he wore blue sweat pants and a t-shirt, and with each step stabbed the asphalt with a six-foot dowel. Slow going, his kind of motion, but the set of his shoulders telegraphed his determination. We spoke about walking. His doctors had told him to get moving and keep moving or else lose the ability, so he walked two or three miles a day, no matter the weather. We parted at the corner of Lillian, where I turned for home and he headed for the upslope of Plumb Lane.

Harold was not only a physical mess, he also didn't feel well enough to maintain his wardrobe or hygiene. More than once I came upon him walking the neighborhood in a blue bathrobe, its front held closed by oversized safety pins. His white athletic socks were sliced open at the top so that they drooped like flower petals around his white calves. I had to wonder whether any local ordinance prohibited the wearing of a bathrobe as an outdoor garment, but I came to doubt it. His robe covered more of his body than would tennis shorts and a polo shirt. Those safety pins, though, they were quite the touch.

Later I learned that when he had the money he bought himself disposable briefs. His washing machine had quit working and he hadn't the cash to get it repaired. When he didn't have the heart to beg a laundry favor from his ex wife he simply ordered new socks, underwear, t-shirts, or pajamas from J.C. Penney and had them delivered to the house. Presto, something clean to wear. He was adaptable, I'll give him that.

Eventually Harold's eighty-year old heart failed. I last spoke with him while he was in the hospital, his final trip to that place. He knew he'd reached the end.

As of this writing he's been dead ten years but I still think of his house on Palisade Drive as "Harold's house," and as I walk the neighborhood I sometimes imagine slowing my steps to his, the *thock ... thock* of his stick marking time as he puts in his miles.

↔

Mid-June ~

A new aide filled in today. There is a certain learning curve to acquainting someone with Momma's routine, her preferences, our kitchen set-up, all the tools and tricks. But these workers are savvy to the idiosyncrasies of elders. This substitute was no exception. I had explained Psycho Dog's propensity to snap, to decide that anyone or everyone is an enemy of the Queen. Momma and Deborah got the day started and seemed on track as I left for a meeting.

Later, Jim positively frothed as he told me: My mother and that dog! She told Deborah that her dog hadn't ever been vicious until we hit her in the face with a rolled up newspaper.

I had to laugh. It's exactly what his mother would say because her perception is that her dog has never needed discipline, never been anything but an angel. Mounting a defense or explaining how her dog was typically a twit during our visits to her home before she moved here would be useless. A person gets something fixed in their thoughts as *truth* and almost any occurrence thereafter can be marshaled to corroborate that position. Standard operating procedure for us all.

A prime example was my grandmother, who annoyed my mother by persisting in certain beliefs. My mother would say (and sometimes wail) "My mother, the liar! She *knows* that's not true." The fact was that Grandma didn't know anything different than what her thoughts, formed by receding memory and logic, conveyed to her. Her perceptions, no matter how ill-conceived or error-filled, were her reality.

Poor Grandma. Poor Mother. There was no resolving their disparate points of view toward life's details. My mother has probably at some point thought that she will never err like her mother did, but I've seen her in action. She can be as forgetful as someone a decade older, misinterpret what others say, and become confused when under the influence of deadlines, decisions, or pain. And though I imagine for myself a special immunity against my mother's inevitable errors (super-immunity bred at the same murky depths as my "I can do it all" perspective) I will likely object to her alleged falsehoods, though hopefully not to her face. No use thinking otherwise.

↔

June continues ~

From *The Wall Street Journal*, "Are You on the Hook for Mother's Nursing-Home Bill?" The piece, by Kelly Greene, says that twenty-nine states have "filial support laws that could be used to go after seniors' adult children for unpaid long-term care bills."

The laws are rarely enforced but they provide facilities the power to pursue financial remedies from the grown children of elders who cannot pay their own way, even when it is not the child's "fault" that the parent incurred said expenses.

So ... for those of us who are medical powers of attorney for our elders, or general powers of attorney, we might do well to keep in mind that we may someday face financial responsibility for our elders' assisted living expenses.

↔

June 18 ~

I suppose I should be glad that after two and a half years, Psycho Dog appears to have quit urinating on Momma's bedroom carpet, yet I should be more careful what I wish for because now the dog wants to be let out of her bedroom in the wee hours (no pun intended). It is as if she has an internal timer because it's almost within the same half-hour every morning. This morning it was four-fucking-fifteen a.m.

↔

A June Friday ~

Today I met my two older brothers in Graeagle, a tiny northern California town where they had been fishing for a couple of days. The town was originally named for a Chief Gray Eagle. Its mining and logging history succumbed long ago to the development of golf courses and their attendant summer homes but it remains at its heart a small town. Think: no stoplights, just a reduced speed limit for the stretch of road that embraces two whole blocks of shopping at its center.

We had dinner at the Coyote Grill. Naturally, talk turned to Mother, whom my middle brother had just returned from visiting. She was been upset about something my youngest brother had written. To paraphrase what he told her: What you decide about someone else's words or tone is entirely up to your interpretation. When you communicate by phone or e-mail, the other party is not there for you to see their expressions. You needn't feel hurt or insulted by words only. You are the one who decides what you think about them; nobody else controls that.

He was talking about a single incident, but his advice could well apply to in-person conversations (which *do* include body language and facial expressions). We choose how we react to what others say. We can automatically take a negative view or allow that it is possible we could be misinterpreting the other person's intent.

I spent the hour's drive home rolling his advice around in my head, trying it on for size.

↔

Late June, a Sunday ~

Momma and Ellen, having walked laps on the deck for Momma's daily constitutional, were sitting in the sun. In the shady zone closest to the house I sat working some stitches into a silk insert for a handbag I'm remodeling. Parts of their conversation were directed at me. Somehow the topic turned to a segment on the nightly network news showing a video clip of an adult school bus monitor being bullied by a bunch of grade school kids.

Momma: A lot of money came in for anti-bullying efforts (She meant the donations that flowed in after the video's release on YouTube).

Ellen concurred.

Momma: What she needed was a baseball bat.

She went on to recount an anecdote about her younger days when kids congregated to play in the open front yards of her neighborhood. The kids from nearby homes all got along pretty well (they would have all been boys playing together; no girls in the mix), but sometimes a couple of the boys from one block over joined in. That's when the high jinks ramped up; play got rowdier and sometimes troubles arose. Always those two boys.

Momma described how one day those boys came over to play and were mixing things up with the younger kids. She went out to set them straight and told them to get out of there.

One of them said she couldn't make them scram.

She told him she was going home to get a baseball bat and he'd better not be there when she got back.

Momma went home, got the weapon, and fooled around a little to give the kid time to make up his mind. When she went back out to check, he was gone. She gave a little chuckle at the memory.

Me: Wait a minute. You think it is okay for an adult to threaten kids with a baseball bat? That's okay to do, but when we wave a rolled up paper at your dog, we're wrong.

Momma was silent.

Me again: Maybe I should get a baseball bat for using with your dog.

Momma: You could do that, but it wouldn't work.

Ellen laughed and Momma chuckled. And that was the end of that conversation.

↔

We have been making plans for a July trip to meet friends in Coeur d'Alene, Idaho. It will be a week away from home for the playing of pinochle and the (re)telling of old college and Army stories plus new stories of grandbabies and home renovations, of travel and work and retirement.

Momma's thoughts are elsewhere. She seems to have absorbed the network news about fires raging in Colorado and decided we should take precautions.

Now she wants us to pack our most valued personal items into Jim's red truck so they'll be safe when our neighborhood becomes an inferno. She imagines that while we are away our pictures, jewelry, and important papers will be lost to a conflagration of multiple homes, old elms, and cedars.

Jim refuses to prepare for a worst case scenario, though mostly he just doesn't cotton to instructions from his mother. I explained to Momma why she need not worry about such an unlikely event, besides which, Ellen's job would be to get them both to safety. They would not be fleeing in his ¾-ton truck, but my little sedan. And besides, any worldly possessions left behind could be replaced or else lived without.

She eventually seemed somewhat appeased, though unfortunately, firestorm stories from other states keep on coming.

↔

Early July ~

Jim: I don't know if I can do many more years of this.

Me: When you can't, just tell your mom we'll move her to assisted living, where she'll see her favorite aides regularly.

Naturally, that's as far as the conversation went; he just needed to vent.

↔

July 8 ~

Tonight's network news broadcast featured the death of actor Ernest Borgnine.

Momma: What was that?

Jim: Ernest Borgnine died at ninety-five.

Momma: Was he old?

Me: Ninety-five. Just a youngster, compared to you.

Momma: Nobody's comparing.

Maybe survival in the face of growing infirmities, dead friends, and a husband lost to his faulty heart is easier if you just stop counting the years and the losses. A person can think themselves younger than they are and perhaps thereby act younger, or else function at a level more young than old.

Like Momma I am a pragmatist and recognize the veracity in her approach. I like nonsense plenty, but a majority of the time I am all for reality. Perhaps that's because my childhood home was directed by parents who never openly discussed any hard truths about raising four children on a single income. All of the truly important topics slept behind a curtain raised and lowered on strings held by adults.

As a consequence I am willing to discuss aloud just about any subject, and to acknowledge the common ground on which we stand as well as the chasms that divide us. I believe we benefit when we openly examine our emotional and physical states and seek information and answers.

↔

Today Jim drove his mom to see her heart doc. Later he related how she had walked in from the disabled parking zone to the elevator bank. Riding up to the fifth floor, Momma reported feeling nauseated but she seemed fine throughout the office visit. Afterwards, she opted out of stopping at the take-out restaurant where she likes to get a dinner of beef and potatoes. Instead they headed home.

Jim said he glanced over at one point to note that his mother was slumped in her seat, her head on her chest. He spoke to her but she didn't answer. He thought to himself, "Maybe this is it," and kept driving. At least he would bring her home.

Before long she roused herself and looked around. He told her what had happened.

When they got home she napped longer than usual then seemed fully recovered. Jim seemed a little unnerved, but not distraught.

I helped Momma into bed for her nap and assisted with her after-nap routine. She showed no obvious negative effects from whatever it was that had happened. Maybe it was the heat, or perhaps her computer brain rebooted itself.

↔

July 23 ~

One day back from our vacation and already Jim has twice cleaned from the carpet what he decided are vomited bits of undigested nuts, gifts from Pickle Dog. After Momma's naptime, he once again counseled her against feeding nuts to her dog. Once again she denied having done so, though we know she shares her snacks that way. She would have felt safe indulging her little love while we vacationed elsewhere, and Ellen would not have stopped her.

Later in the day Jim found a nut on the carpet that had leapt to safety from Momma's sofa. Had he looked he would have found others beneath the cushions. A scavenger of morsels, our big dog always detours to Momma's place at the dining table when he comes into the house. We keep Stanley Steemer, the carpet and furniture cleaners, not exactly on speed dial, but on our calendar.

↔

July 30 ~

Momma looked down the table toward me and asked: Did you see the newspaper today with all that talk of nonsense?

Me: Who was talking nonsense?

Momma: That man who would be president.

This being 2012, she was referring to Mitt Romney. She plans to vote for his Democratic opponent because she walks a fairly straight party line. I don't know that she's missed any national elections since she began voting. Nowadays we three go together, Momma's and my votes canceling out Jim's. Jim jokes sometimes about assisting her in the voting booth by pointing her eraser at the candidates of *his* choice. He'd never do that, though. Too honest.

I had to smile at Momma's choice of words. Sometimes she cracks me up.

↔

I'm about to reveal my crusty side by declaring that most people who would swear on a stack of bibles that they love their in-laws the same as their own parents are exaggerating in the service of kindness. It is not out of love that you turn your home into an assisted living facility for your in-laws with yourself as staff, it's out of either a sense of duty, or as in my case—respect. Also, a willingness to provide some measure of dignity to an elder whose last years are sending postcards from closer and closer addresses.

Out of true love you might tend people born of your womb or your heart—a child you carried for nine months and then gave birth to, a spouse who has been your lightning. But not for the person who cooked an occasional holiday dinner, financed a bit of college expenses, or was often interested in what new film you saw this week. Whether he or she is truly friendly or merely benign, that person is not *of* you, they are just part of life's bargain.

I subscribe to there being degrees of separation between us and the people we know, and sometimes between us and the people we love. So too there are degrees of separation between caring about a person's safety and wellbeing and loving them like your own.

When my mother moved east to tend her parents (note the plural), she chose to perform ten thousand acts of kindness for a mother she once described as "not much of a mother," and a father who flat-out abandoned the family when she was young. I can see how, though frustrated by the demands of tending people she may not have actually liked, she felt bound to them by love and loyalty.

There are other people who would find joy in our current arrangement, in the constant physical and cognitive tending, but I do not feel joy. Joy is what a person feels at giving birth, or perhaps finding God. What I feel is capable and willing, and most days relatively satisfied.

↔

Early August ~

My eldest brother told me today that when he called Mother she was suffering a massive headache. It's the third or fourth time. I know it worries her, which means it is higher on her prayer list too.

He will visit her soon, so he'll drive her to the doctor or dentist or whatever is needed. She is not always good about tending to her own health. I'm not sure why that is except that when we were young she always put us kids first; that's where our family's modest resources went. Like the rest of us she has probably imagined herself invincible so that when a random health challenge strikes she can't quite figure out how to address it.

↔

Here's one of my favorite elder stories from recent times: A long-time friend of ours hails from the Pacific Northwest. Her parents still live there, her mother now beset by Alzheimer's and her father doing his best as Tender. So far they have remained in their home together.

This friend flies north at intervals to stay with her mother while her father takes a break from providing care by visiting his grown children. She told me recently that her mother has been known to report that she is 90 when in fact she's only 80, and also that she used to be a spy.

You have to love that—that at some point the facts just don't hold weight like they used to, and that our realities shift while seeming no less real. If that elder now thinks she was once a spy, that's good enough. Why attempt to convince her otherwise? She faces no danger from counterintelligence operatives; not one person could think she possesses secrets of national import. In fact, since fiction requires creating characters who are extraordinary in their skills and pursuits, her imagined life might inspire a character for the next bestselling novel.

↔

Mid-August ~

Today Momma came to the breakfast table dressed in an outfit that demonstrates her problematic eyesight: bright, salmon-colored pants with a red, white, and blue striped blouse, topped by a dusty orange vest. The colors were loud enough that she could see them, but frankly, the combination made my sinuses ache.

One of the aides had chosen the ensemble; Momma never dresses herself since she cannot reach the garments in her closet. When I later helped her to bed I used my laundress's prerogative to toss those pants in the laundry basket, thus breaking up the crazed combination.

Momma said as she struggled to undo her blouse buttons, "I don't remember this blouse." I explained that she'd worn it last summer too, having ordered it from one of the catalogs she favors. Noticing how she is losing her grasp on many everyday details makes me want to memorize the important things surrounding me: how the morning sun splashes across the hardwood planks of our living room floor; our backyard's variations on green; the electric snap of one humming bird scolding the others over cylinders of sugar water; the hollow at the back of my husband's waist, and his long, long legs.

As I sit typing this, the neighbor's lawn sprinklers are ratcheting a tune in the evening air and an angry hornet is buzzing circles inside a yellow trap hung from our oldest apricot tree (50 years and counting). We arrange a cruel end for stinging creatures.

↔

August continues ~

While working on this memoir I traveled to the California coast to clear my head and enjoy what I think of as a time out from, well, *you know*. I calculated that a getaway could include time for me to review my journal notes and that alone would feel like progress. It turned out that the only period when my car wasn't needed for Momma-transport or other commitments was the week of my birthday.

Only once or twice have we made a to-do over our birthdays. There was my thirtieth when Jim conspired with a girlfriend of mine to throw a surprise party, inviting co-workers and softball friends. I happened to have the flu that day but we went for our usual walk after work. When we returned home our house was full of revelers. I still have a few snapshots showing the fun of that celebration, and also how young we were. Almost a decade later I threw a dinner party for Jim's 50th.

I haven't ever needed banquets or heaps of gifts. I'm allergic to fragrances and don't count my self esteem in diamonds. Also not necessary: a trip to Paris, New York, or San Francisco to commemorate any particular day of the year. I would rather travel somewhere marvelous because it is Tuesday, or else to meet up with friends.

I was delighted to plan a break from tending duties while getting to choose exactly where to spend my time off. That it was my birthday week was mostly irrelevant. I say *mostly* because last year Jim offered to invite a couple of people over for dinner and I declined. It wasn't that I don't acknowledge my age—I am turning 57 as this goes to print—it's that given the choice, I wouldn't spend my birthday organizing a larger than usual meal, cleaning house in advance, prepping for dinner, cooking, serving, cleaning up afterwards, and, oh yes, tending to Momma and her dog during what is supposed to be a special evening in my honor.

For some reason Jim didn't understand "No," "No thanks," and "Really, I don't want a birthday dinner." Instead, he invited his daughter and her boyfriend, people we care about and with whom we regularly share family events, ballgames, and dinners. Maybe he felt they represented outside forces that would inject an extra upbeat into the monotony of our dinner routine. How do you tell someone not to invite their daughter to Sunday dinner? I didn't know how else to say No.

We planned, we cleaned, we prepped. I cried before our guests arrived, then washed my face. We cooked and served, we cleaned up afterwards. The conversation was pleasant, the evening went well, but I was physically exhausted from the extra work, and emotionally spent by the thought that I couldn't even opt out of extra duties on my own birthday. What kind of a life had this become?

Maybe last year's reality made it easier for me to choose my birthday week for a getaway this year. I would tend to no one but myself.

The drive to Fort Bragg turned out to be shorter than I had calculated. I arrived on the coast at about 6:00 p.m. and took a room at The Beachcomber motel with a view to the waves pounding against the town's western edge. In a downtown restaurant I had a delicious fish dinner and a nice glass of wine. I slept well.

The next morning I went to the lobby, which doubled as a breakfast room for what they billed as "Continental Breakfast," an American version that Europeans would find laughable. Entering ahead of me were what looked to be two little old men. But, no. One *was* white-haired and a little stooped (perhaps 80), the other was a younger man of indeterminate age. Together they shuffled toward the counter that held a display of sweet rolls. I stepped into place behind them. The younger, beefier one swung around and fixed me with a disfigured gaze.

I smiled at him and said: Hello.

He spoke around two front teeth that protruded from his mouth like chisels: Hi!

He said something else that was hard to understand but I made out the word "car."

Me: I have a car. It's outside.

Him: What (something indistinguishable) it?

Me: It's white.

Him: What *kind*?

Me: It's an Audi.

With a crooked smile, he sighed, less a signal of satisfaction regarding a particular brand, *Ah, an Audi,* and more like I had named an object of independence and brave travel that a lucky person might control. His eyes followed me until we separated with our plates of pastries.

 The two men sat at a table near mine, the older man repeatedly prompting the younger one to eat his banana. Then a lady entered the room and joined them. Silently I constructed a family for the three of them—she as the mother of the younger man, and the older man as her father. Three generations headed somewhere, with two older generations tending the younger one who lit up at the thought of a car, any car.

 How long had they been traveling their specific path, and how far their destination? I found it easy to parse for them a story spun of milkweed with a beginning, middle, and end constituting pure conjecture, but I am fairly certain of one thing—theirs has already been a longer, tougher journey than mine, and they have miles yet to go.

↔

 A friend of mine is a hardworking casino executive. Never a moment's rest at work, but she says that when she's off duty she can let go of details and the need to organize everyone and everything around her.

 Her father died last year and today she told me she still feels guilty about whether she could have done more for him. She had always kept in touch, always visited him in California. When he fell ill she flew or drove to his hometown to arrange for his care. When his health deteriorated further she spent her weekends visiting him and coordinating his hospital and nursing care. Then the doctors told her that he would not live long. He wanted to go home, so she arranged for that too.

 This friend was working 50-60 hour weeks and dashing back and forth until near the very end when she told her bosses that she would be by her father's side for the duration. It might be a week, two weeks, or three. So it was that she was at his side when he died at home but she still wonders if she could have done more. Had she spent more time at the hospital or at his bedside, would he have survived longer? Her brain tells her *No* but her heart poses questions that go bump in the night. She feels guilty for not having arranged for some detail that she cannot even name. She wishes he could signal her from the other side to let her know that he's okay. If only he would.

Now her godfather is in declining health and wants God to take him. He's in a group home in the city where he spent his adult years, well tended and in remarkably good health for an 89-year-old, but he would like to be done with it all.

My friend sounds satisfied that she has done right by her godfather; he made choices that she executed on his behalf. But the doubts she harbors about how she took care of her father ... that's a whole different thing.

↔

Dear CJ,

Isn't it something that you and I make a pair who can count their friendship in decades? When I was young I marveled at adults who had known people for twenty or thirty years. Such calculations made them seem kind of ... *old*. Also, I couldn't fathom people who weren't married (which held all sorts of implications) actually *liking* each other for a lifetime, but here we are.

I see now how days accumulate into years, throughout jobs lost and gained, the changing of relationships and home addresses, the arrival and departure of step-children, and always, our mutual affection like a perennial shrub adding yet more blooms each year.

We may never share the windblown beauty of an outing under sail, an autumn campfire in the high desert, or another delicious day at Nob Hill Spa (and thanks again for that), but we will, I hope, convene at PJ's for another three hundred brunches, lunches, and conversations about places well traveled, the multiple personalities of art glass, the vagaries of writing, and all the other large and small stuff of life.

I hope someday we shake our heads over the decades we have to our credit and agree that they've held a goodly share of moments that others can only wish for.

↔

Went with a friend to see the film The Best Exotic Marigold Hotel, with a story set in Jaipur, India. All witty British dialogue and a plot that broke the theater audience into laughter. In this flick, senior citizen Brits and Americans go abroad for bargain prices in living out their remaining years. Along the way there are various misunderstandings and attempts at feeling sexy, or useful, or that one hasn't lived a life in vain, plus reversals of fortune, and one marriage in its end-stage. I haven't laughed that hard during a movie in years. When I described the plot to Momma she frowned, either in concentration, or distaste.

Maybe you had to see it on the big screen to appreciate it.

↔

When one of the aides arrives in the morning I always feel relief. It's not like I fear getting stuck with morning duty. I've done plenty of morning duty. I guess it's that I feel lucky to be in a position to have a few hours' worth of assistance each day. There are many who do without.

Oh, I grouse. Usually about someone's tardiness, lack of attention to detail, or how I sometimes end up cleaning up after one aide or the other. But mostly, as long as Momma is safe and has someone to read the newspaper headlines to, I feel okay about things.

It takes iron patience to perform tending work—the glacial pace, the repetition, the messes. Our regular aides each have a decade or so of experience at this. Two of them have worked for an assisted living facility and one has "lived in" while providing care. When they are not tending to Momma they are performing similar work elsewhere, which means that almost every single day of the week they deal with people in various states of disrepair and/or who are angry, forgetful, lonely, sloppy, demanding, and there must be a few who express appreciation.

Not many people would excel at working as a personal attendant. Many do it, even I could do it, but few are made of the right stuff to excel at it. Personal attendant is just one occupation that would not suit me for the long haul. Others include special education teacher, waitressing, childcare, data input, neurosurgery. Not that I couldn't figure most of them out on a strictly temporary basis; they just wouldn't suit me, nor I them.

Tending work often gets dismissed as unimportant, or beneath one's dignity. When someone insinuates that, I think, "Really?" It's not that it's not good enough for other people (or for me either) but that most people are not capable.

The way I see it, occupational Tenders are in parallel positions to school teachers, who practically raise today's children because of how many parents are largely absent. They are disciplinarians, mentors, support systems, moral compasses, and they deliver the goods. While they do the really hard work, year in and year out, the rest of us are practically skating.

↔

We won't ever own a saloon or bar, but if one ever becomes the hangout of Tenders, they might serve cocktails with these names:

A Whole Night's Sleep
Dream Vacation
Pick Me Up

What Do You Call This?
Biding My Time

Symptom of Something Suspicious
A Long, Dry Spell

↔

September ~

For Momma's 98th birthday dinner I applied her makeup (with gray eyebrows, not green) and off we went to Simon's Restaurant where we met a few relatives and friends. There she ordered her favorite dining-out dish— sautéed frog's legs. You've heard of teacup poodles? A frog's legs resemble the legs of a teacup chicken.

As the light streaming through the restaurant blinds faded away, Momma fingered items on her plate before deciding which deserved the next bite. In the low light she could not make out the sentiments on any of the birthday cards, nor the details of the gifts brought by nieces and dear Margie, a longtime friend and Eastern Star compatriot.

My husband asked what advice she had to share after 98 years of life. Momma put her finger to her chin and said: When they tell you about the golden years, this isn't them.

We all chuckled and clucked.

She added: The golden years are from about forty to sixty, or seventy. Those are the good ones.

She was right, I'm sure. She had passed beyond those radiant times to arrive on the dimmer side, which as it turned out was still of this earth.

We put her gifts aside for the pleasure of looking at them tomorrow. Wearable items will go into dresser drawers and edible stuff will be left out for snacking or desserts. Later she will say, "I don't remember how I got those."

I'm not sure the old wisdom holds true that a person will need less money to live on when he grows old. There might be a period where all is calm, where all a person wants in the morning is a slice of buttery toast and a cup of coffee. Well, and a television that works, and maybe an extra blanket on the bed. But then something changes and simple things don't seem so simple anymore.

Soon you've accumulated a cane, then a walker. An electric can opener, rails on the toilet and tub, and a bench to sit on while showering. A helper to squirt the toothpaste.

One of those rotating car seat cushions for more easily climbing in and out. A driver to take you places.

Wash and wear clothing and comfy shoes. Someone to do your laundry.

Microwave mac and cheese, home delivery of groceries. A willing cook.

Life takes on variations of the help we once received as infants and toddlers. Think: stroller, bouncy seat, babysitters, a stepstool at the sink, assistance with bathing.

The items and helpers who make late life easier cost considerably more than toast with a spoonful of that creamed honey my grandmother Ruby so favored. Better start saving up.

↔

September 3 ~

Jim described a conversation he had with his mother today that included how she's been living with us for 2-1/2 years now. He told her that she will reach the three-year mark this coming January. His report was meant to prepare me for hearing the same question from her when I helped her get ready for bed, and that's exactly how it worked.

Momma, pulling on her flowered pink pajama top: I just can't believe I've been here for three years. That's what Jim said.

Darn brooms were no help at all

I explained how long it's actually been and that we don't reach year three until January. She said she didn't remember what had brought her here. I described her fall inside her garage that November evening as she returned from taking out the trash. She didn't remember.

I mentioned the trip to Urgent Care for x-rays. She nodded.

Me: You said it felt like someone pulled on you from behind.

Momma: It was like someone pushed me.

Me: But you fell backwards and flung your arms out.

Momma: There were two or three brooms in the corner. I thought they'd break my fall.

So she *did* recall the brooms and the tumble backwards upon the brick and concrete steps, but not spending time at our house afterwards before returning home, or the morning roughly 45 days later when she couldn't get out of bed for the pain in her back, or the subsequent surgery and rehab followed by a return to our house, or her conversations with us when we talked about whether she should go home again. The details would simply not rise up for her.

I summarized her decision not to go home again and the six months her house sat unoccupied before she decided it could be rented out. And the giant yard sale and the moving into her bedroom here of that coffee table she likes so much. The round side table, the happy Buddha, the vases and knickknacks too.

She sighed, as if what I'd said made it seem more real, like it might have happened just that way. Then she offered: Well. Thanks for taking me in.

That's the first time I had heard that from her. She has never said she is glad to be here, or that things have worked out okay, or that she feels safe and fed and tended to.

I told her we are doing the best we can, even if we don't always get along with her dog. She nodded. The rest was small talk. For some reason I felt like we had crossed a line that had divided us this whole time.

↔

September 9 ~

Friend Peg called me today in response to a rambling phone message I'd left for her a week or two ago. I just wanted her to hear my voice, to know that I'm in her camp, whatever she's going through—the treatment, the workplace stuff, all of it. She said that she feels good. It had been three months since she'd been to her oncologist and though she's due for another scan, the treatment she's been on seems to be working at containing her lung cancer.

She sounded great, making plans to retire with 31 years, 30 of them earned and one she had purchased a while back. Her husband has retired in order to spend more time with her but she keeps going to work each day, plus she serves in an employees' union and organizes national conferences for a group she belongs to. Her pace as a cancer patient would make many a healthy person weep.

We talked for a while about this and that, and I promised I would keep sending crazy cards and leaving wordy voice messages that her answering machine cuts short, and when we rang off I felt uplifted. If I ever feel blue, she'd be a good one to talk with.

↔

We're giving up foods now. Not in the pursuit of slimmer waistlines, though that would be to my benefit, but because they're dropping off Momma's greatest hits parade. Every time I turn around there's another something that gives her a stomach ache, or "doesn't taste as good as I remember." Or, the meat was too tough to chew, or we discovered that it incites loose bowels.

For as intelligent and lucid as Momma is, it seems that she cannot conceive that the basics of one's existence do not remain static; change is in our life's DNA. She doesn't any longer go dancing, drive a car, or mow the lawn; she can't perambulate without a walker or a wheelchair. She would acknowledge that all of those things have changed, but for some reason there are roadblocks in her mind about food.

Did I mention elsewhere that chocolate can act as a laxative? Momma said recently when I cautioned her against eating lots of Hershey's kisses, "Maybe they've changed the way they make chocolate."

That's it! Let's blame the manufacturers and chefs. We have many to spread the blame among because there are other things *they've* changed: spaghetti sauce, fibrous vegetables, most all cuts of beef, BLT sandwiches, Chinese food, and Kentucky Fried Chicken.

↔

I have homicide in mind, or maybe dog-i-cide. Such thoughts arose when I opened the family room shutters this morning to find a great gob of dog vomit, partly on Momma's loveseat and the remainder on the recently cleaned carpeting below.

I set about clearing the mess with a paper towel and left the vacuuming and scrubbing for later. Then I went into Momma's room. Before I took her commode bucket to dump I suggested she quit feeding her little hairy friend the mixed nuts and potato chips she snacks on while watching television.

Me: She's not a person. She's a dog.

The Rat looked out at me from her spot beneath Momma's soft, warm covers. She didn't growl but I bet she wanted to. That dog enjoys the privileges of a lover, sharing Momma's bed, sitting beside her to watch TV, laying across her lap for the reading of the newspaper.

In response to the news of barf-in-the-morning, Momma said: I'm sorry.

I wanted to say, "You're not sorry enough to quit feeding that crap to your dog. If she dies from eating that stuff, you'll be sorry but I won't." I wanted to say that but I didn't.

↔

Dear JJ,

You thought I stopped loving you, or that you had done something to chase me away. Not at all. My problem was that you left no doubt about your moral requirements for the men you dated. I assumed you expected the same of the man you would marry. It turned out that I knew about him what you did not.

I tried pretending otherwise until in my hypocrisy I could no longer look you in the eye. I am sure he adored you, adores you still, and rightly so. I just couldn't pretend that he was as perfect as you thought.

My choices came down to truth-telling versus walking away; one would paint me cruel, the other faithless.

I have missed you, and when I stop to think about the people I have lost, I count you among the good ones that got away.

↔

I've been reading more and more in the popular media about the changing demographic and economic realities for younger generations of Americans, and the projected likelihood that our children and grandchildren will find it harder than we did to achieve financial independence through accumulating wealth or assets.

In our respective families, our parents, Momma included, earned more and accumulated more than their parents. We did the same. Our daughter, older than the Millennial (those born between 1980 and 1990) accumulated both education and work experience before America's Great Recession of the late 2000s. An only child, she stands to inherit from more than one relative, so she will likely avoid true financial hardship.

My nieces, on the other hand, are in their twenties and have at times struggled to secure steady, full-time work. That makes it less likely that they will save enough loot for the rainy days that are yet to come.

Though ours is a culture that has not much practiced multi-generational adult living, we have been reading about young people moving back into their parents' homes. I wonder now whether these re-blended families portend a future increase in family caregiving by the Millennials whose parents who provided longer for their children than did earlier generations. America's protracted recession may be what tips our culture toward a future resembling historical times when grandparents, their children, and their grandchildren lived together and provided for each other.

↔

More September ~

Arriving in the kitchen after helping his mother to bed, Jim said: You know, we're going to both be crazy before this is done.

Me: So, we must be half-crazy by now?

Jim: Yeah.

Me: I don't feel crazy. Numb That's what it feels like.

He paused, then: Maybe that's it. And you know ... she might make it to a hundred and ten.

Me: We've been taking good care of her, so she might.

He blinked hard before walking away.

At about 1:45 a.m. Momma rang her bell for Pickle Dog duty. I gave Jim a push and he got up. I was lying awake when the bell rang again at 2:30 a.m. so I took a turn.

At 3:00 a.m. I heard the lawn sprinklers come on, followed twenty minutes later by the first hiss of the drip system. At 5:00 both zones ran again. I was falling asleep, or trying to, when Jim began to snore. I gave him a shove to make him roll over.

At 6:00 Momma's bell rang again

I nudged Jim, who gave a groan and got up. The big dog followed, expecting breakfast.

At 7:00, Jim's alarm went off and he rose to prepare for his day of golf.

At about 7:45 he came in and kissed me goodbye. I rolled over to catch a few last winks.

At 8:05 the bell rang again from Momma's room and I rose to let Pickle Dog out for her fourth pee.

As I write this it's about 11:30 a.m. and there's a rhythm section marching in circles behind my eyes. I'm waiting in the Goodyear Tire shop, surrounded by the aroma of new rubber and coffee going stale in the bottom of the pot. My plan is to have the tires on my car rotated, in case, you know, I need to flee my home life (just kidding, I think).

At some point in the last month I told Momma that when Pickle Dog's kidneys get to the point where she is going out three or four times a night, we'll have to figure out some other arrangement.

Me: We can't go on like that.

She agreed: Yes, that would be too much.

I don't hold out hope that she'll remember that conversation. When I told Jim about it he shook his head and said: That's going to be hard.

↔

I've been giving more thought to some of the newspaper and magazine articles that address the high costs of care for the infirm, which usually means elders. *USAA Magazine* ran a nice first-person story about a 37-year-old daughter whose 71-year-old father moved in with her to share expenses. They split most of the bills and though they had had awkward moments, they were adapting to their new circumstances and even finding pleasure in spending time together again. The piece cited 51 million Americans as living in multi-generational households. That's about twenty percent.

That young woman's father is not infirm. But someday he might be (or she might be) and they will adjust their circumstances once again. This has got me thinking about how instead of mandatory military service, maybe young people ought to be conscripted into a national program providing eldercare.

I know that sounds weird, but what if a young person could earn a portion of their own future care by working for two or three years in a senior living community or care center? People could contribute physical energy and mind power in advance. This would be similar to the way national service programs train people to work with underserved populations and communities, this one being specifically for the good old U.S.A.

Some workers would be suited to administrative work, gathering data, or writing software, while others would engineer adaptive aids or work as artists in residence. Still others would scrub floors and cook meals. We could call it Peace for Seniors Corps or Volunteers in Service to Infirm Americans.

I suppose we'd need another President Kennedy to make it happen, and how likely is that?

↔

September continues ~

Bowling has started up again, making my repaired left knee cranky but lifting my spirits each time I drive away from the house toward two and a half hours across town with friends. Wednesdays bring the ladies' league where we play poker as we progress through the frames. I have grown fond of the Breezy Mountain women, some of whom have been bowling together for over 30 years.

On Fridays I also bowl with a good friend, her son, and her son's best friend. Last year was our first year fielding what is called a mixed team, and it was fun, though daunting to be bowling against so many high-scoring men on the opposing teams. Two of last year's teams did not return this year, but one of the new teams contains an 86-year old woman who resembles the aging rocker David Crosby, with similar wispy white hair but no mustache.

When it's her turn, Millie teeters up to the line in slow motion and gives her ball a roll. Damn if she doesn't sometimes roll a strike. When that happens she turns toward the seats, gnarled fingers tipped by thick gray nails held up in surprise. That slow grin, such delight! Her fans go wild, offering high fives all around and they cheer her louder than for any other bowler. The rest of us say things like, "When I'm 86 I hope I'm still bowling."

↔

Late September ~

Okay. So we're giving up on the pain patches that we said we would fight for. Momma's insurance carrier is going to win out against a 98-year old because the FDA approved Lidoderm for two conditions—diabetic neuropathy and post-herpetic neuralgia—not for spines crippled by osteoarthritis and osteoporosis. Not for the sake of quality of life and walking a few yards, or using a wheelchair each day. For the ability to rise slowly in the late morning for a breakfast of grapefruit, cereal, and coffee cake. For one dinner out per year with a friend or two, and the inevitable medical appointments for eyes and bones and heart.

Back in August they had provided one last three-month approval and warned they would cease benefits for this prescription as of October 1. The doctor's assistant assures us that the insurance company need not acquiesce to another extension. If only Momma had diabetes or was suffering the painful effects of shingles. Then her insurance would cover her pain patches. Poor Momma. She's not sick enough.

We will adjust to this new setback, and so will she. We've become adept at the adapting and adjusting of routines and expectations. It's a Tender's variation on evolution—instead of expecting the least fit to expire, we enlist whatever resources we can to reasonably ensure the health of our least fit. I'm talking about Momma.

↔

Early November ~

Ding dong, The Rat is gone.

There's a story behind her demise, which goes like this: For nine days in October, Jim was roughly 1,200 miles away, hunting pheasants with three friends.

While he was away I rose three or four times each night to let Psycho Dog out to pee in the yard. Sometimes she dashed out and tended to business before hurrying back in. Other times she walked around sniffing virtually every blade of grass plus many of the leaves littering the ground.

At least once in recent memory she wandered around for a handful of minutes before looking up startled, as if finding herself in a foreign land, perhaps delivered there by aliens. Wide-eyed, she dashed for the spot where I stood propped half-asleep against the doorframe. She had accomplished no dog business.

Those nine nights while Jim was away transformed me into a very unhappy dog mutterer who multiple times each day curses about one lightweight daffy dog. We had reached an impasse—it became *The dog versus me.*

I gave Jim two days to unpack and settle once again into our routine before I provided my conclusion, one he had surely been anticipating for some time.

Me: I am done with the dog.

He knew which canine I meant. He nodded and said: Does it have to be today or can I think about how to handle it?

I set no particular timeframe but conveyed that he should field the multiple night duty calls until we found a resolution. We tapped our veterinarian for tests, advice, and commiseration. The eventual assessment of The Rat amounted to: advanced old age (much longer than average), reduced vision, almost complete hearing loss, kidneys in fail-mode, and dementia. It was time.

When Jim brought her dog home from having overnight tests, Momma cried. She had thought that Gin-Gin was gone for good. That would come soon enough. We explained the nature of the dog's infirmities and that we needed mercy for her and for us. Momma reluctantly agreed, but of course she was devastated. Fourteen years gone like that, in what must have seemed an instant.

Momma cried more for her dog's demise than for her only brother's death a while back. My logic is that her brother was thrust into her family circle by sources beyond her control, but Pickle Dog had been her chosen friend.

In the first few days following her dog's departure, Momma resisted taking her afternoon naps. We understood. She was missing her accomplice for undercover work.

Things have evened out since Jim left with Pickle Dog and came back without her. I am sleeping better than at almost any time in the last few years. That will change, of course, with Momma's inevitable further decline. If there's anything I know it's that our home life will continue to change, then change some more. Change is the one sure thing. Until that next phase, though, I am feeling once again like I can do this, like we can do this together. In the meantime I sleep a deep, dream-filled sleep.

↔

Mid-January – the conclusion of year three ~

My notes don't reflect what we were chuckling about, probably some disconnect in a conversation with Momma while helping her to bed.

Me: I won't ever do anything wacky.
Jim: Nope. Me either. I'll never be strange.
We looked at each other and broke into laughter.

↔

This is the point at which I should neatly summarize the lessons Jim and I have learned. He and I are not at the end of our tending journey so I can only provide my impressions of our progress to date.

We vastly overestimated our capacity for tolerance and patience while underestimating how many adjustments we would expect of his mother. Smarts are no match for eldercare. They help, but more important is patience. Throw in some creative problem-solving and a willingness to seek help when you need it and you might succeed.

We waited far too long for that first in-depth debriefing about how we were faring (meaning how *I* was faring). Though at this point we're approaching equilibrium, I should have insisted sooner on a more equitable division of duties.

I think we both chafe a bit less at the fusty routines populating our days and have become better communicators, which I hope will enhance our marriage when we need to tend each other.

I finally let go of some of my need to "do it all." Some days I ignore the accumulating dog hair or leave our bathroom unscrubbed just a little longer. And too, I've grown a bit kinder. Instead of killing spiders that take a wrong turn into our house, I might breathe deeply and escort them unmolested back to the garden.

About cooking: I suspect I overstated my distaste for standing at a hot stove. Somehow I have a binder full of recipes that when I prepared them the first time came out both delicious and pretty on the plate. Clearly there were times, before eldercare, when I enjoyed a bit of kitchen play. Some future day I might take it up again.

Jim has assumed a greater share of the tending duties and also begun baking the chocolate chip cookies he loves, amazing us both with how yummy they are.

Since it's in my nature to make things into bigger projects, I turned my journals into this memoir, which proved cathartic.

Now that I am getting a full night's sleep I once again probably run the risk of sounding overconfident when I tell you that although at first it felt like eldercare might prove the undoing of our happy home, we are still putt-putting along. And though I expect tougher days to lie ahead, in fact I'm sure of it ... I remain optimistic.

↔

Dear Mother,

I possess a spotty memory of my childhood years. Other people can call up two hundred Technicolor scenes from past decades while I carry around just disconnected snapshot impressions. Perhaps I am an unreliable witness.

Certain details remain clear, though—for instance, your determination. Dad stayed for as long as he did because you fought for us to remain a family and held on tight, the way you thought a parent should. You loved us; some mothers do not. The things you did for love; we were the lucky ones.

I remember your compassion for others. Just by proximity we kids should have absorbed that quality from you. I wonder now whether you ever received the compassion you needed, and whether the yes or no of it shaped your faith and your personal conduct.

I think of those early years as fleeting, even though while living them they seemed to pass in slow motion. Each important marker stood at a great remove toward which we rushed headlong—the next weekend, next summer vacation, next birthday. We were always in a hurry while you were likely not. More likely, you savored every small milestone, the minutia of those years of wonder and exploration, every new word, every step, each scribble and scrap. The chalk, the dolls, the tricycles, pebbles, Army men, baseballs, books.

Remember the craft projects? You were an artist at heart, untrained but inspired. I carry your love of art and a pinch of your talent. Given the chance, would you have pursued a career in art? Had there been money for classes or tutors or art supplies, and just a single inspiring mentor, could you have realized your artistic potential?

You put all of your energies and heart into raising four kids—a Herculean task. And we turned out fine. Not perfect, of course, but fine, carrying with us the effects of your considerable efforts.

These are the words that come to mind for describing the young-mother you: fiercely protective and loving; rules-oriented; classically beautiful; no-nonsense Christian; fashion conscious; hardworking; pioneering feminist-traditionalist; racially colorblind; honorable and generous; moral; compassionate.

I have recently been pondering which of my own traits might reflect credit on you. I count: honesty; a strong work ethic; advocacy for equal rights; respect for diverse races and ethnicities; a love of children; a passion for learning and the arts; and liberal politics. All characteristics I am pleased to possess. It turns out that even if in other ways we are miles apart, in these things we are alike. That thought makes me feel grateful and a little awed.

I am trying to learn resilience so as to be a better daughter-friend to you. Were I a different person I might pray for guidance. But since I believe I am the leader of my own parade, I will undoubtedly continue to struggle with the evolution of our relationship. I rarely make promises intended for collection at some far-future date, but this one I offer willingly: You never gave up on us; in turn, I will stand by you.

↔

I am trying to imagine other helpful information from our home to yours, learned through trial and error, and sometimes error and error. Of course we're only experts on matters relating to our own family and our part in it.

I can't prescribe how you might build a case for assisted living or arrange your life to bring your elder into your home, but you might learn from our strategies and thereby help your family members face their post-golden years. It also might help your planning process to cite an acknowledged, if narrowly defined, expert. To that end: I acknowledge my expertise at tending and you may cite my advice to your heart's content.

Wishing you satisfaction in tending, and always, in all ways, peace.

Products that Work for Us

We have employed the following products while tending or assisting various elders. Many of these virtually duplicate those used in assisted living facilities and may keep your elder(s) safe in their home or allow them to adapt to living in your home.

Clothing/Shoes/Accessories

~ **Lightweight wash-and-wear garments**, including sweaters or jackets and sleeveless vests. We choose blouses or shirts with buttons that can be worked by arthritic fingers (no pullovers), and elastic-waist knit pants.

Women are prone to polyester. I don't know why. I'm guessing it's because its known for being wrinkle-free, practically indestructible, and women are so often the directors of home-laundry.

Polyester washes well; it can be dried at a low temperature or hung. Unless it's woven into high performance athletic wear, though, it doesn't breathe well, so choose cotton or blends containing cotton for hot weather wear, as they are less likely to aid and abet heat rash (we know this from personal experience). A cotton-poly blend can work well and may be labeled as permanent press.

~ **Button-front shirts and blouses** work best for a person who dresses while in a chair. Momma is petite, but she needs roomy clothing that accommodates how a body spreads at the hips when seated. We buy her the same size tops and bottoms she wore in her robust, early years.

~ **Let's talk underwear.** Momma wears her undies low on her hips, just below her belly. She seems to like the cotton-blend high cut styles I choose for her, which allow movement where one's legs meet one's torso and do not bind when a person sits for long periods. When a person's back or hips are sensitive to pain, full briefs may put persistent, if gentle, pressure on lower back muscles. As long as they stay in place, looser undergarments may also work better for men.

~ **Thin, soft cotton socks** keep feet warmer than synthetic knee-high stockings or trouser socks, but shoes need to accommodate them.

~ **Non-slip shoes** with Velcro closures make getting dressed easier for an elder and/or the person who tends them.

Momma's toes had hurt her for years. She probably thought such discomfort naturally came with aging, but in fact her feet had widened and lengthened over time and she had not shopped for shoes in years.

Because the ends of her toes jammed against the insides of her favorite ancient loafers, her toenails lifted and thickened from the trauma. With shoes that fit properly, her feet are now happier.

She likes Skechers brand, which offers a number of stylish finishes, wide openings, and secure fasteners.

We have not shopped for men's shoes that are easy-on but I'm sure they are out there somewhere.

~ **Large-face watch** with bold numbers. In the name of adaptation we switched Momma to a watchband with a Velcro closure.

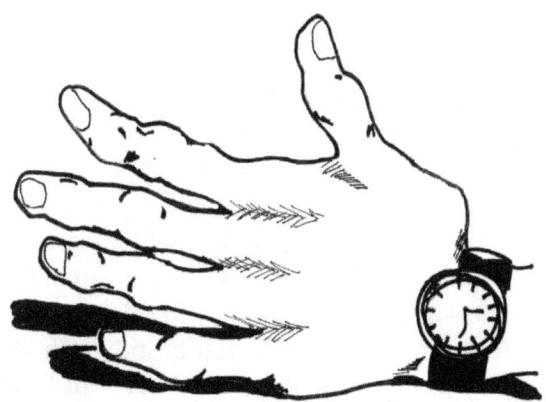

We also installed an extra large kitchen clock.

Health & Hygiene

~ **Lightweight, warm blankets** – Easy to layer in the cold season, and light enough that an elder can maneuver while in bed or exiting. Fluffy synthetic blankets trap air for warmth. They dry quicker than cotton or wool but might not be bleachable.

~ **Bedside commode** – Like so many products, these have adjustable legs and handrails for support. HINT: Add a dash of liquid dish soap to a few inches of water in the waste bucket to moderate odors when the commode is used. Flush waste products down the toilet, of course! Then fill the empty bucket with hot, soapy water and a bit of bleach and leave it soaking in the bathtub between uses.

~ **Shower wand** – Non-elders like these too. We chose one that is lightweight enough for Momma to use with assistance.

At the bedside, Momma receives what one aide calls a PT&A (Pits, Tits, and Ass) wash. A bowl of warm water and a washcloth does the job. We insist Momma shower at least once a week, and on that day an aide washes her hair at the sink and rolls it into curlers.

~ **Gentle bath soap** – We like Aloe Vesta brand soap that comes in an easy-to-handle bottle. Their rinse-free version is extra gentle.

~ **Power toothbrush** – Not just for kids! They do the back-and-forth work for the user.

My mother would be smart to use one of these because her teeth are falling into disrepair. When she needed to have a tooth pulled, the dentist recommended a Waterpik. She tried it briefly but was afraid it would jump off the counter so she quit trying. A year or two later she was back having another tooth pulled.

~ **Alternating pressure mattress pad** – The one Momma uses is an Aero-Pulse by Medline. It operates with a small, plug-in motor, and cycles through gentle inflation and deflation to ease the pressure on torso and limbs while in bed. It goes under the bottom bed sheet. A doctor may prescribe this product for delivery by a medical supply company, though it might not be covered by Medicare.

~ **Disposable hand wipes/baby wipes** – Good for many body parts. We buy the fragrance-free version.

~ **Flushable wipes** – We first saw Pure Touch brand Tush Wipes used in hospital care. They have a slight fragrance, come individually wrapped, and are handy for travel or home use.

~ **Disposable vinyl gloves** – Similar to the kind used in dentist offices and hospitals. Available at drug stores; you might also find them in your favorite food market. Home health aides consistently wear hand protection while assisting with bathing and cleaning duties. This is to guard against the transmission of bacteria present in body fluids and solids, and to keep the elder safe from health challenges the caregiver may possess.

~ **Washable, bleachable bed pads** protect a mattress from being soiled. A pad can be sandwiched beneath the bottom bed sheet, or if used atop the bottom sheet, can be employed for the moving of an immobile person (you'll see this tactic used in nursing homes and hospitals). *Disposable* **bed pads** may be useful if bowel incontinence is a problem.

~ **Disposable paper panties** – Our name for what others call adult diapers. The pull-on kind work for ambulatory users; the kind with adhesive tabs work better for users who are immobile. FYI: Temporary urinary incontinence may follow injury to the spine or surgical procedures that affect the spine or nerves nearby.

~ **Panty-liners, or pantiliners** – The same styles and brands used for menstrual cycles do duty for incontinence protection and come in a range of protective styles.

~ **Compression stockings** can be purchased at many drugstores or big box stores. They help keep fluid from pooling in the legs of people with poor circulation. These can be a trick to pull on so we use a device we purchased from a medical supplier.

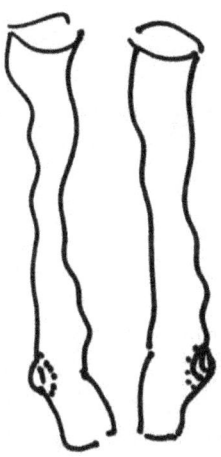

Men's and women's sizes are based on height though I have yet to see any for truly short people. We buy a medium size for Momma, but they extend higher than her knees so we fold down the top few inches. A doctor may recommend these, but they are sold without a prescription.

~ **Disposable face cleaning cloths** – I started using these to keep from having to bleach Momma's washcloths after she cleansed her face of makeup, but have since realized that hand wipes make a good substitute when dotted with a bit of face soap.

~ **Fragrance-free products** – Since everyone in our family suffers from allergies, we use as many fragrance-free products as possible: Seventh Generation liquid dish soap, Arm & Hammer and All laundry detergent, and Downy fabric softener. We use Basis bar soap and Dr. Bonner's "baby-mild" castile soap (for the cleanest rinse). We all feel better when not impersonating the characters Congested, Sniffly, or Weepy.

~ **Roll-on pain gel** – We use a capsaicin product available by mail order—Glucosamine Brand Pain Relief Roll-on Gel made by Concept Laboratories. When I tried it, my skin felt on fire, but Momma thinks it's great. The roller ball head allows its easy application to just the right spot.

~ **Calcium alginate wound dressing** – for weeping wounds. Senior skin tears easily. If heart congestion is present, fluid that pools in the legs can spontaneously break through the skin. This dressing stops the weeping and does not require a prescription (be sure to read the instructions).

~ **Laxatives** – Use these with care. They can be helpful for short-term comfort, but used daily they may reduce a person's control of their bowels. An alternative might be glycerin suppositories which are applied directly to (in) the problem area.

~ **To moderate loose bowels**, try applesauce (apples naturally contain pectin, a binding agent). Cooked white rice mixed with cottage cheese might help, but dairy products are not for the lactose intolerant among us. See "Milk substitutes" on the next page.

~ **Manicure/pedicure** – Nail clippers and emery boards come in a variety of styles. I find that Momma's toenails are difficult to cut without first soaking them in warm, soapy water.

When she lived alone, she bought a battery-operated tool for sanding her toenails, but never used it. I have seen a podiatrist use a similar device, much like a battery powered Dremel tool; it takes the length off in no time flat. I have put Momma's aside in case we someday need it for refinishing furniture.

~ **Clothing protection while eating** – Oh, the crumbs and spills and bits of food that go everywhere! People using wheelchairs may not lean far enough forward to keep their crumbs on the plate or table. Momma uses a hand towel to cover her lap but bits of food still end up in her clothing. We have talked about trying the full-coverage bib-type protectors in use at the last rehab center she spent time in; they are available at some retail pharmacies. I reckon some day we will need them.

~ **Diminutive flatware** – Age brings diminished strength, so those heavy crystal glasses that sparkle like diamonds might look fabulous on your table but are unwieldy for hands that cannot safely grip them. Arthritic hands need small utensils, drinking glasses, and cups. This might not be the case for a man with large but arthritic hands.

Momma uses juice glasses (never full-size glasses), salad forks, tiny fruit spoons, and a small serrated knife (Victorinox™ brand) that will cut through any food we serve her.

~ **Food quirks** – Due to having worn teeth, Momma does what Jim calls "squirreling." She fills her mouth with five or six bites of food and begins to chew, adding another bite or two each time she swallows a portion.

One holiday, I was closest to her when she began choking. Upon my firm instructions, she spat out a mouthful of partially chewed food. She was fine immediately afterwards and I have yet to attempt a Heimlich maneuver.

~ **Salt substitutes** are for users with hypertension (high blood pressure). This product tastes like chemicals to me, but Momma pours it in a stream onto her food and says it's fine.

~ **Milk substitutes** take the place of dairy (cow's) milk. FYI: lactose intolerance can produce stomach or intestinal distress and diarrhea (or very loose bowels). And if your senior is a vegan, he or she may prefer to avoid animal products anyway. Momma had troubles of the former persuasion so I switched her to soy milk, containing plenty of protein compared to rice milk, which has almost none.

Elaborating further, "dairy" means any product made from cow's milk, including hard and soft cheeses, ice cream, whipping cream, table cream, half-and-half, cream cheese, cottage cheese, yogurt, and butter. Some lactose intolerant people can tolerate a bit of yogurt. Because they contain fewer milk sugars (the milk's proteins) and are mostly fat, I can tolerate butter in moderation and an occasional spoonful of cream cheese or whipped cream.

Substitutes for cow's milk cheeses include goat cheeses, which have a distinctly different taste. I've seen yogurts made from other sources; coconut milk or the like.

~ **Spicy and pickled foods** – As her senses have waned, Momma developed a taste for horseradish and pickled foods. I take no insult that she wants horseradish for dipping all meats and sometimes even vegetables.

She also likes anything sweet (supposedly, the ability to taste "sweet" is the last to go). Momma adds sugar to her presweetened cereal and piles it onto her daily half-grapefruit. Luckily, she is not diabetic.

~ **Chlorine bleach** – As mentioned elsewhere, we add a portion of bleach to the commode bucket when we soak it between uses. Unless you like that holey look favored by teenagers, do not pour bleach directly onto clothing, even when it is floating in water. Mix bleach with your wash water before adding any items.

~ **Counter wipes for disinfecting** – Handy for cleaning the handrails of a commode, toilet, walker, wheelchair, and for wiping counters and toilet seats, which we do almost daily. We find that house brands work as well as national brands.

Safety

~ **Chairs with arms** provide stability for sitting or rising. There are even chairs employing an embedded electrical motor that slowly stand a person upright, especially useful for people with weak limbs.

~ **Necklace-style call button** – These operate on a remote signal between a special telephone receiver-sending unit and the transmitter necklace worn by the elder. Most have a generous range so that a signal from outside the house can be detected. The call center notifies your designated responders, such as family members, neighbors, or emergency personnel. You will likely find a service in your community providing 24-hour response for a monthly subscription.

Momma subscribed to this type of service when she lived at home. She used it twice for urgent medical response. Had she not ever needed it, we still would have enjoyed better peace of mind knowing she could.

~ **Room (baby) monitors** might safeguard elders who only need to speak up to be heard from another room. For elders who wander, look for attachable alarms that fit on a doorframe and sound off when that door is opened.

~ **Grab bars** – Not just for the tub, but useful alongside doorways or within hallways where there are no other grab points. Most are installed using anchors and screws, but there is at least one style that employs suction for attaching inside the bathtub or shower stall. Check for likely locations, including near steps into or out of the house and garage. Available at big box stores, major drugstore chains, and home improvement centers.

~ **Toilet rails/riser** – Handrails are easily applied to a toilet fixture, providing safety for a person while sitting or rising. They come in a variety of styles and can be purchased at major drugstores and home improvement centers. Some require no tools at all, just a little elbow grease.

A **riser** is attached between the porcelain bowl and the toilet seat to shorten the distance the knees must bend. There are different styles of these, too, available wherever health and home improvement items are sold.

~ **Bathtub bench or chair** – Sturdy but lightweight, these have rubber feet and come in a variety of styles to fit tubs and showers.

~ **Tub side handhold** – In her home my mother installed a sturdy handhold that attaches to the tub without tools. This spare style may not work for a tub enclosed by shower doors. Available at big box stores, major drugstores, and home improvement centers.

~ **Hospital-style bed** – These come with or without side rails, those tubular supports meant to impede a person's fall from a bed or provide leverage for entering, exiting, and shifting around. This type of bed comes in manual and electric styles for elevating the head or foot.

Momma's primary physician prescribed hers, but such a bed might be available to rent or lease from a medical supply retailer.

Entertainment

~ **Large print books and magazines** – Even if Momma weren't legally blind, large print materials would be easier on her aged eyes. With standard size newspaper print she uses a magnifier to read headlines but can rarely make out the stories themselves.

~ **Vision aids** – Technically, eyeglasses are vision aids, but there are myriad styles of handheld magnifiers and lightweight plastic reading panes that magnify whole paragraphs or pages.

Optometrists can write orders for **special prescriptive eyeglass lenses**. A bit of searching around will turn up more OTC options.

We also find that a **desk lamp with a flexible neck** allows Momma to shine a bright light on her book or meal.

~ **TV Ears** – A clever name-brand device for individualizing your TV's volume control. The transmitter plugs into your TV, sending volume to the lightweight receiving earpieces worn by the user. You can mute the sound while your elder cranks up the volume to her ears. These can cost as much as $90 at electronics retailers. Standard headphone styles may cost less but weigh more.

Mobility

~ **Four-legged cane** – This cane's feet will have rubber tips and its trunk will be adjustable to a user's height. Its four legs are configured into one straight side and one splayed side. The straight side goes closest to the user.

~ **Four-wheeled walker** – You've seen these advertised. They may be purchased online, from big box drugstores, or from medical supply retailers. There may be heavy-duty versions for hefty users. Four-wheelers come with brakes and seats, and some styles have a basket tucked beneath the seat. Medical supply retailers will "fit" a walker to its user, and occupational therapists can train users in how to step up onto or down from a stoop or porch.

~ **Standard Wheelchair** – Many of us have accumulated leftover safety equipment from friends and family members (my friend KH jokes about operating a lending program for used mobility and safety equipment from her garage). In truth, a wheelchair works best when fitted to the user and a therapist can provide tips on safe use.

Momma purchased a gel-filled seat cushion which has a washable zippered cover. She reports that it is an improvement over the standard wheelchair seat, which is waterproof but unpadded.

~ **Public transit for the disabled** – Most large cities and some smaller cities employ special buses for the transport of travelers who are disabled. Access to these special vehicles and their specially trained drivers generally requires registration with the transit agency using authorization from a physician. Your senior can access this service whether living with you or not. Simply ask her physician to make the referral.

~ **Useful automobile features** – Older autos with bench seats were the easiest for Momma to enter and exit. For some reason, bucket seats are not as accommodating.

Seniors who are auto drivers might prefer a vehicle which sits high enough for a person not to "fall" into. While we're on the subject, most elders would probably benefit from a senior driving safety course. If your elder has been regularly knocking the side mirrors off his auto, you have the perfect conversation starter.

Easing Into Providing Care

Late life can be a messy, somewhat helpless stage paralleling our entrance into this world. When it comes to tending, our family has not done it all or seen it all, but some of what we have learned may help you arrive at a reasonable plan for obtaining care for your elder or providing it yourself. For instance, we eased into eldercare rather than arriving with our hair on fire. That's not to say that we won't see sparks in the future.

~ **Seniors will underestimate** the amount of help they need. Even after we had been performing such duties at her longtime home because she no longer could, Momma would report keeping her own house, tending the yard, and washing her own laundry. She was recounting activities she could *remember*.

Boomers probably underestimate how much they accomplish too, but the evidence reveals yard services, housekeepers, tree trimmers, car washers, hair stylists, manicurists, and more, kept busy by medium-oldish people who don't want to (and can't) do it all themselves.

~ **Communication, communication, communication.** As early and openly as possible, talk with your family elders about their wishes for their future care. Be honest in your appraisal of what you can and cannot provide for them. Not everyone is suited to provide hands-on care for an elder, let alone a disabled elder. If you can, begin these conversations during your elder's "Golden Years," before infirmities overwhelm them or you.

~ **Seek consensus** from family members (including your elders) when making plans. Identify who will provide which types of assistance and how that assistance will be paid for, scheduled, and/or delivered. Reassess the plan with them at regular intervals.

~ **Consult neighbors and friends** about their favorite products and their approach to solving problems. They might also serve as someone to vent to when the going gets tough. Jim has cousins who will provide us with an evening's respite. You might search out a caregivers' support group. Someone there is bound to have experience with the ideas or tactics you've been searching for.

~ **Consider your elder's pet** and how it will fit into your household scheme and schedule. There are "rescue" groups for almost all breeds of cats and dogs. You may need to find that pet an adoptive home and allow its master to first grieve the loss, then adjust to life without a fuzzy friend.

~ **Keep a calendar** of appointments, social dates, and scheduled home maintenance that can be referenced easily. This can help an elder feel more secure in knowing what the coming week or month holds. My mother provided her parents with a calendar that duplicated the one steering her actions on their behalf, helping them remain attuned to their own affairs.

~ **Lists are good too.** We write out questions we want to ask Momma's doctor during routine visits, and keep a current list of her prescriptions and supplements at the ready.

~ **Adaptive living** might mean setting items on a counter where they can be easily identified and accessed. The older a senior, the more likely they will want bottles and jars lined up on the bathroom counter, and oft-used small appliances and dinnerware left out in the kitchen. In her home, Momma hung clothing items on doorknobs and over furniture. She used and reused the same cup, plate, and bowl on a daily basis, washing them by hand and using her dishwasher for larger items. By keeping things simple (and therefore easy), she managed on her own for many years.

~ **Routines** invariably provide peace of mind through predictability. You might not be in a position to drastically alter your household routines, but they will have to shift in order to accommodate another person, even someone you know well (even someone you assist in their own home).

Various aspects of home life might need recalibration. Like to walk around in the nude, eat dinner at midnight, or make love on the dining room table? I'm just saying ... something's going to give.

~ **Choose your battles.** I don't know anyone in their 50s, 60s, or 70s, who doesn't prefer autonomy when making decisions about their own living arrangements, medical care, or choice of companions. For as long as it's feasible, elders are entitled to autonomy too. Health and safety may be the only concerns that need your immediate attention, while other matters are best addressed by your elder. A reasonable approach might be, "Let's try that and see how it works for you." When things work out, that's great. When they don't, it may be time to propose other options.

~ **Slow down.** I move more slowly in my 50s than in my 40s. Ditto regarding my 30s. Imagine being 80 or 90, then slow your pace accordingly, and dial back the setting on your trip wire. Anger might provide a moment's release, but anger alone rarely brings answers. Frustration is another response that won't trump creative problem solving. You can assume that many changes will meet with resistance and small environmental or nutritional improvements may take time to yield positive results. Remember to breathe.

~ **Express gratitude.** Jim and I say things like "You put the trash bin out? Thanks!" or, "Thanks for staying home so I could go to lunch with Pokey." When Momma directs my attention to an article in the newspaper, I acknowledge her thoughtfulness.

~ **Home healthcare aides** could be your new best friends. Arranging an aide for a senior who lives in their own home might keep that senior both healthy and living in their home.

When shopping for a bonded home healthcare agency, interview the coordinator from more than one and ask for references (which you then check). The coordinator should gather details about your elder's capabilities, mental acuity, and preferences, and record the answers. In theory, the agency will match an aide's skills and personality to your elder's needs, but in reality you simply might be assigned a worker who is available. Sometimes that's enough.

Aides can assist with bathing, meals, shopping, and light housework. Some are not allowed to dispense medications. The agency we work with trains their personnel in many relevant subjects and requires them to know First Aid and emergency procedures.

Eventually, agency management should ask how the aide assigned to your elder is performing, and you should feel empowered to request a change of personnel, if needed.

~ **When moving an elder into your home**, try to bring their most important personal items because there is comfort in the familiar.

We brought all of Momma's jewelry, personal paperwork (including multiple address books) and useful small pieces of furniture. She drinks hot cocoa from her own Franciscan ware cups and soy milk from her own juice glasses. Her morning grapefruit arrives in a familiar bowl, and come dinner we sometimes use her serving pieces.

Momma: Did you bring my good straw hat?
Me: It's right here. Did you want to wear it today?
Momma: No

Momma's vintage fur stoles and a favorite red coat reside in a storage closet in our home. She hasn't worn them in thirty years or more but I have pulled them out to prove that they are safe.

~ **Threadbare clothing** is no crime. In spite of owning dozens of newer blouses, Momma's favorites for knocking about are her oldest shirts that long ago wore through at the cuffs and elbows. Being frugal she had cut off the ragged parts and hemmed the sleeves shorter. Lightweight as cobwebs, they remain her preferred tops during hot summer weather. When someday her bosom or spine shows through we will retire them.

~ **Allow your senior to contribute** to your household and their own upkeep by deed and/or financially. Allow for physical contributions to be slow or imperfect. If the dishes get done but it takes twice as long as when you do them, does that count as a problem? Not in my world.

~ **Your elder's food choices** will differ from yours even though you grew up eating some of those same dishes. And, as you likely know, digestive health can falter over time. Dairy products and rich foods (especially fatty foods) that younger people enjoy with impunity may cause digestive upset for elders. Certain medications can too.

Plain food plus fresh fruits and veggies might improve an elder's cholesterol, digestion, or weight issues. And keep in mind that as the years pass it becomes harder to detect thirst, so encourage your elder to drink more water.

There's also the challenge of how much to help with cutting food into bite-sized pieces. Because Momma sees poorly and can't chew through tough or fibrous foods, we cut them into small bites before we deliver her plate to the table. It's been a gradual process with little discussion. In increments we shifted the line we were crossing each time we crossed it.

~ **Get real about body parts and their functions**, which include stomach, bowels, and the urinary tract. Boomers' parents may not have openly discussed sex, menopause, or doctoring. Get comfortable with gently and directly discussing personal cleanliness and the avoidance of bacterial problems that arise with poor toileting or hygiene practices. Anglo-Americans probably bathe more than other ethnic groups, and old people simply smell different; some accommodation is in order. But severe cases of poor hygiene might lead to a serious infection—an outcome to be avoided.

~ **An elder's temperature gauge** may be faulty. You might need to direct the use of layered clothing and to make hydration a priority. Momma cannot tell when she is overheated until she is sweaty. This can lead to heat rash. The back and seat of a wheelchair admit no air, so that's one body zone where heat- and moisture-related skin problems can erupt.

~ **It's never too early for grab bars,** shower aids, and other safety measures, whether your elder lives in their home or with you. Having dependable safety aids may help your elder stay longer in his or her own home.

~ **Occupational and physical therapy** are designed to keep a person functioning optimally through capitalizing on a person's strengths, with a focus on safety. The PTs and OTs Momma has worked with through the years have kept her thinking about safe walker and wheelchair use. In some ways she believes those experts more than she does us.

~ **Home and personal safety** may prove a challenge if an elder's hearing is poor. Even though we've all been conditioned to dial 9-1-1 for help, the phone may be out of reach after a fall. That's when a safety necklace with a call button could save the day. Check for special window stickers meant to alert first responders to an occupant's use of oxygen or other special needs.

~ **Seniors may fall for scams.** Not just internet scams but phone scams. We know someone whose lonely father has sent hundreds, if not thousands, of dollars to Nigerians who call to chat, and guess what? The senior has control of his own finances and willingly sends personal checks to the recipients. Repeated explanations and warnings have been for naught, so the family's new challenge will be keeping the father safe and solvent, which may include convincing him to move into assisted living where his phone number will change.

~ **Library programs** provide audio and large print books, and might sell used books at bargain prices. Ask a public librarian about any free or low-cost local or federal programs providing audio books for the blind or disabled.

~ **Respite** is when a caregiver takes a break from tending duties. Your community might offer a "senior day program," which might include lunch, socializing, and table games or other activities. Enrollment may cost a few dollars per day, but there may be subsidies for low-income seniors. Our county senior services division also offers mental health counseling.

Assisted living and nursing facilities provide residential respite care. The elder checks in for a day or two (or more) and the facility's staff provides them with daily living assistance as needed. It's a little like hotel living without a 5-star spa or 24-hour room service. This might prove a handy resource to assure the health and safety of an elder while the Tender(s) vacations.

If your elder doesn't need assisted living, but a safe, social place while you're away, you might query the "independent living" residences in your community. If they have unoccupied units, they might on a temporary basis rent out accommodations with meal privileges in the company of other seniors.

Alternatively, a home healthcare agency can provide 24-hour live-in care for virtually any period.

~ **Hospice care** applies to life's end, usually the last six months to one year. Our local hospice program is a fee-based program affiliated with a hospital. It employs nurses who will coordinate pain care and nourishment for physical comfort. There are also trained volunteers for in-home assistance such as keeping a vigil and/or performing non-medical duties (even grocery shopping). Such a program might provide services at a reduced cost for low-income seniors.

~ **Review supplemental insurance and long-term care poli-**

cies. Most of these insurance policies provide benefits that pay a fraction of the going rate for long-term (nursing) care. Long-term facilities provide health care aides, cleaning staff, meals, laundry, occupational and physical therapists, nursing staff, and a physician who supervises medical care and may respond to minor emergencies. Rates fluctuate widely between cities.

Some long-term care policies provide for a bit of in-home care, but only through certified home nursing agencies.

Some Medicare supplemental health insurance policies provide for a year of long-term care benefits after a hospital stay of at least three days followed by thirty days of long-term nursing care that has been paid out of pocket. The benefits are generally fixed and are based on current Medicare requirements, generally room and board plus various types of therapy.

In her mid-60s, my grandmother purchased a policy that ended up benefiting her greatly in her 90s. As it turned out, the value of the benefits paid on her behalf during her final three or four years of life roughly equaled the premiums she had paid for all those decades.

~ **Geriatric physicians** are not necessarily old practitioners (but doesn't that term sound like it?). They are doctors specializing in health issues pertinent to the aging process. Perhaps the proper term is geriatrician. Unless your elder already has a competent physician who knows them well, you might seek a geriatric specialist. Some even make house calls for the very infirm or aged.

Attend doctor visits with your senior but allow him or her to answer the doctor's questions; that's one way a physician assesses cognitive functioning. If your senior's records show you as an authorized contact (this may require a special release), you can request copies of medical records, communicate concerns in person or by phone, and consult their physician confidentially, when appropriate.

~ **Medical Directive.** Each senior should have one of these, but Tenders should too. This is a one-page declaration of a person's preferences regarding the prolonging of life by extraordinary means. Your physician's office or local hospital may have a form you can use, probably for free. This allows a family member to honor their elder's wishes when it comes to a catastrophic or terminal health event. Plan to file a copy with the senior's primary care physician and carry another in the auto typically used for transportation.

A separate matter is establishing a medical power of attorney (POA), which legally assigns an agent to make health decisions in the event a person cannot make their own. Jim and I are both named on Momma's medical POA, which was drawn up by our family attorney. Legal services for acquiring this type of document might be available to low-income seniors through a "senior law project" in your community.

~ **Keep a journal or diary.** You might not plan to write a memoir but you could find it helpful to vent a little on the page, so to speak. You can always shred those pages later, your frustrations dissipating as those itty bitty slices of paper go into the recycle bin.

~ **Get enough sleep.** There is no substitute for adequate rest. We were wrong to play servant to Momma's little dog for as long as we did because doing so deprived us of sleep for nights on end. We thought we were being kind to Momma and Pickle Dog, but it's nearly impossible to be gracious, thoughtful, useful, and communicative when your head feels stuffed with cotton.

Some day Momma will need to ring for us in the night and I'll go back to being "the listener," but for now I spend the dark hours in snooze mode.

~ **Take time for yourself.** Small pleasures count for a lot: meditate, try a new craft, take a walk, sit in the shade and watch your garden grow. Any little thing that brings you satisfaction will ease the day's chores and obligations.

~ **Exercise!** You know that old axiom "move it or lose it." I'm trying to keep moving now in the hopes that my post-golden years will prove mobile as well.

~ **Maintain friendships** and as many outside interests as you reasonably can; this also applies to your elder. If your lunches or dinners or movies out get curtailed, pick up the phone to remain connected to people who support you, especially those who don't always want favors from you. Populate your universe with people who treat you with respect.

~ **Delegate the hosting of holiday meals.** Maybe you're a glutton for doing it all (a habit I'm trying to break), but if you are the lavatory attendant, social secretary, personal dresser, makeup artist, and chauffer, someone else can manage chef duties, yes? As we say in our household whenever anyone else performs a necessary chore, "It's just the way we like it."

~ **Admit when you need help.** Secure assistance from other family members, or hire outside help for some of the daily duties. The other side of this coin is to admit when your elder needs to live elsewhere, such as in assisted living. In that event, you have not failed him or her; that's just life. We can each only perform a certain amount of hands-on care, which in some cases might include no hands-on care at all.

~ **Toileting—a touchy subject.** We have it on good authority that bowel and/or urinary incontinence is the primary cause for elders moving into assisted living facilities. There may be no anticipating just how much you can tolerate in that regard, but it might help you to think of your elder as someone with a terminal illness. That bit of rephrasing might soften your perspective.

If your elder takes hypertension medication ("water pills"), more frequent urination will result. The good news is that frequent trips to the bathroom may help train a body to do its business in a timely fashion.

We have developed a toileting routine which we try to maintain throughout the day, and have adopted certain word choices referring to it. We say, "Let's go down the hall before dinner" instead of "Do you need to use the bathroom before dinner?" This saves on interruptions to meals or accidents that occur from waiting too long.

If you and your elder can be matter-of-fact about infirmities or challenges, the tending process may prove less distasteful and tote smaller emotional baggage. Your management of toileting challenges through patience and routine might help your elder function well in your home.

~ **Learn the signs of a stroke**, which results when the blood supply is cut off to a portion of the brain. According to the National Stroke Association, the following are potential signs of a stroke:

1) Sudden, unexplained confusion, or difficulty understanding or speaking; 2) A numbness or weakness of the face, arm or leg, especially when present on just one side of the body; 3) Vision problems in one or both eyes; 4) Dizziness, loss of coordination or difficulty walking; 5) Severe headache with no known cause.

High blood pressure increases the risk as do other factors. Treat a possible stroke as a serious medical emergency.

~ **Buy stock in paper goods.** Just kidding. We joke about this because we seem to be constantly buying facial tissue and toilet paper. We also go through a lot of paper towels, which we like to think helps us avoid acquiring or spreading cold and flu viruses.

~ **Your elder's universe** will likely become richer through joining your home but smaller through leaving the arrangements they previously knew. They may ask about the smallest details of your day because their days no longer contain such texture.

~ **Eschew perfection.** There is no such thing, and attempting perfection can wear you out. Trial and error may suffice for working the kinks out of how most tasks work. To paraphrase Michael J. Fox (in *AARP Magazine*) and apply his words to fit our purpose: Our happiness grows in direct proportion to our acceptance of our situation, and inversely in proportion to our expectations.

Lower your expectations of yourself and others. Then when things work better than anticipated, do an internal end-zone dance and pour a celebratory cocktail. A sip of *I Told You So*, anyone?

~ **Give yourself permission** to be confident, followed by uncertain; regularly surprised; and to change things that need changing.

~ **Medicare has a toll-free phone line** where real people answer questions about coverage and benefits. Through that office I once obtained information I then used to challenge a denial of supplemental insurance benefits. We recouped $26,000 in benefits owed my grandmother.

~ **Reduce prescription costs** by asking the doctor for samples of medications being prescribed, and whether generic versions will suffice. Also discuss any OTC (over-the-counter) medications or supplements in use at home, as some may negatively interact with prescription meds. Your pharmacist is another good source of information about contraindications, side effects, and alternative OTC products.

~ **Request financial relief** from eye care or other medical specialists. They may have policies for discounting out-of-pocket fees and co-pays for low-income seniors. Likewise, non-profit hospitals are required to discount their fees for low-income patients, but consumers must ask for such concessions. If your community has a university school of medicine, the campus might also house an outreach clinic that serves uninsured or underinsured patients.

~ **Affordable housing** for seniors may be available in your community. Our county's senior services division provides listings of senior-friendly (or subsidized) housing.

~ **Federal dollars** are available for qualifying seniors to carry a cell phone that will dial 9-1-1, or that is loaded with prepaid minutes for basic communications. Even if your elder lives with you, he or she may qualify for this subsidized program. Check with your county's senior center.

∞

There. I've shared almost all I know, unless you yearn to propagate peonies from seed or sew a perfect French seam. As for tending, a year from now we will be awaiting a letter containing birthday wishes from the U.S. president to our centenarian. Between now and then we will likely have learned a couple or a dozen more lessons.

Employing a bit of creative license, I left out most of our wrinkles when drawing Momma, Jim, and myself. Just saving on ink (*ahem*).

If you were wondering about Momma's given name, it's Hazel, which she never uses. Instead, she uses her middle name, which I recently learned was chosen by her passionate-for-pink aunt Ennie, who plucked it from a novel set in France. I smile every time I think about that.

∞

About the Author

By now you have figured out that with my husband I've been providing care to my mother-in-law for many years. The first phase took place at her home down the street and around the corner from us. The recent 3+ years-and-counting have been in our home.

My intent is for *Postcards* to deliver some useful ideas and a smile to its readers. If you bought a copy online, I hope you'll post a review there. Or send me some feedback through the email address on my website: www.pjoriley.com.

In spite of all my tending experience, I'd like to think it doesn't define me. Since 2001 I've been publishing freelance stories and photos (byline Paula Riley). They've appeared in a variety of local and regional newspapers and magazines, so far none of them about eldercare.

What's great about being a freelancer is that unless you're a specialist, say focusing on medical technology, you get a taste of many divergent subjects while meeting lots of interesting folks. While it's nice to put a story "to bed," for me discovering stories and bringing them to life is always about the journey, literally and figuratively. I like experiencing a destination, a special event, an artist, business, or business person, with a view toward uncovering what's hidden beneath the surface. It's gratifying when it works out that way.

Freelance work varies. It's not all articles and ghost-writing. Because I spent almost two decades in the marketing and advertising biz, I occasionally produce marketing materials for hire. I also worked as an investigator of child abuse and neglect. Between that kind of work and tending, I feel like I'll never be flummoxed by what the human body can withstand or by how people treat each other.

In the last many years my focus has taken a turn toward book projects, thus my first memoir and now this book, which is part personal story and part how-to. Next up? Fiction, a craft I've been studying and practicing.

I won't be the first to say that fabricating a solid fictional tale doesn't come easy. My own background in social work taught me to think in terms of mediating conflict. But, an absence of conflict makes for a boring read, so I've been practicing letting the seams out a little on my natural inclination toward order and pragmatism. I promise that if you sample my next book, a novel, you'll find it contains characters that don't follow the rules and aren't necessarily nice to each other. How's that for a switch from tending?

Thanks for your readership,

Paula

∞

My Darling,
When it's time for us to say goodbye, hold me close and know that I am glad for our long and loving ride. It won't have been nearly enough because it's the good stuff we wish would last forever.

∞

www.ingramcontent.com/pod-product-compliance
Lightning Source LLC
Chambersburg PA
CBHW031358040426
42444CB00005B/335